THE FUTURE-READY CHALLENGE

Improve Student Outcomes in 18 Weeks

L. ROBERT FURMAN

International Society for Technology in Education
PORTLAND, OREGON • ARLINGTON, VIRGINIA

The Future-Ready Challenge
Improve Student Outcomes in 18 Weeks
L. Robert Furman

Acquisitions Editor: *Valerie Witte*
Editor: *Emily Reed*
Production Manager: *Christine Longmuir*
Copy Editor: *Kristin Landon*
Proofreader: *Ann Skaugset*
Book Design and Production: *Kim McGovern*
Cover Design: *Edwin Ouellette*

Library of Congress Cataloging-in-Publication Data
Names: Furman, L. Robert, author.
Title: The future ready challenge : improve student outcomes in
    18 weeks / L. Robert Furman.
Description: First edition. | Portland, Oregon : International Society for
    Technology in Education, [2017] | Includes bibliographical references.
Identifiers: LCCN 2016055933 (print) | LCCN 2017002379 (ebook)
    | ISBN 9781564843852 (pbk.) | ISBN 9781564846198 (mobi) | ISBN
    9781564846204 (epub) | ISBN 9781564846211 (pdf)
Subjects: LCSH: Motivation in education. | School improvement
    programs.
Classification: LCC LB1065 .F825 2017 (print) | LCC LB1065 (ebook) |
    DDC 370.15/4—dc23
LC record available at https://lccn.loc.gov/2016055933

First Edition
ISBN: 978-1-56484-385-2
Ebook version available

Printed in the United States of America
ISTE® is a registered trademark of the International Society for
Technology in Education.

About ISTE

The International Society for Technology in Education (ISTE) is the premier nonprofit organization serving educators and education leaders committed to empowering connected learners in a connected world. ISTE serves more than 100,000 education stakeholders throughout the world.

ISTE's innovative offerings include the ISTE Conference & Expo, one of the biggest, most comprehensive ed tech events in the world—as well as the widely adopted ISTE Standards for learning, teaching and leading in the digital age and a robust suite of professional learning resources, including webinars, online courses, consulting services for schools and districts, books, and peer-reviewed journals and publications. Visit iste.org to learn more.

Also by the Author

Instructional Technology Tools: A Professional Development Plan (iUniverse, 2012)

Technology, Reading & Digital Literacy: Strategies to Engage the Reluctant Reader (ISTE, 2015)

Related ISTE Titles

Innovation Age Learning: Empowering Students by Empowering Teachers, by Sharon "Sam" Sakai-Miller

To see all books available from ISTE, visit iste.org/resources.

About the Author

L. Robert Furman is principal at South Park Elementary Center in South Park, Pennsylvania, where he lives with his wife, Tiffeni, and two boys, Luke and Kyle. Prior to coming to South Park, Furman was an assistant middle school principal for Gateway School District in Monroeville, Pennsylvania.

Through the years, Furman has developed a keen interest in technology, and he constantly attempts to infuse instructional technology into school curriculum to enhance student learning. In 2011, he wrote *Instructional Technology Tools: A Professional Development Plan* and began speaking about the subject at state and national technology conferences. Furman blended his interests in technology and reading, and became passionate about supporting students with literature.

Furman began his teaching career as a music educator after graduating from West Virginia University in 1995. Music was his first love and remained an important part of his life as he continued his educational studies at Duquesne University in the Department of Supervision and Administration where he earned a doctorate in Educational Leadership.

Beyond speaking at venues across the country, Furman is also a contributing blogger for The Huffington Post as well as the Ed Tech Review. He also hosts a well-known YouTube educational video blog called The Seditionists and iTunes Podcast #EduRevolution. Further, he has received several prestigious awards, such as being named in the National School Board Association's "20 To Watch" in technology education and a *Pittsburgh Tribune-Review* News Maker of the Year award.

Acknowledgments

I would like to express my gratitude to the many people who have been instrumental in helping me as I conceived the idea of a book embracing the future. First and foremost I want to thank my wife, Tiffeni, for her constant support and motivation. I thank my children, Luke and Kyle, for always bringing joy into my world, and I thank my parents for their constant presence in my life.

I have nothing but gratitude for our family friend, Dr. Catherine Luke, who enrolled me in the World Future Society and sparked my curiosity and interest in the subject of the future and how it applies to education.

To my Fellow Seditionist, Keith Reeves, I give both my thanks and admiration for always being a part of the discussion on how to change education to be future ready. Our conversations always broaden my thinking.

I would like to thank what I call my "South Park Dream Team", including Carol Lupo, Karen Macko, Bev Jones, Kim Mosi, Kari Havel, and Ellisen Lowe for their continual support in and out of the school setting. I cannot begin to tell you how much your friendship means to me.

A special thanks to Rebecca Turley who continues to help me find the right words to express my thoughts. You are the queen of patience.

I give my thanks to those colleagues willing to share their future-ready ideas with the world: Matthew Jones, Beth Poluszejko, Laurie Brierton, Amy Cramer, Sarah Manly, Barb Levitt, Shad Wachter, and Amy Pryor. You are examples of what's right in education.

I also want to thank all those colleagues who have been with me over the many years and continue to positively impact my life.

Finally, I offer my heartfelt thanks to God for my health, my happiness, and my family.

Dedication

To my two sons, Luke and Kyle Furman. They are always able to bring joy to my life. I am so proud of their abilities to be innovative in all situations. I dedicate this book to my sons and those individuals in their lives who have always supported innovative thinking.

To Mike Kasula, my cousin and Godfather to my son. He has taught my children how to be innovative thinkers in the outdoors and in real life situations. Their love and appreciation for nature is due to his love and his family values.

To my father, Bob Furman. Grandpap has always been a "forward thinker." His philosophy that "nothing is impossible" has shown Luke and Kyle the value of thinking outside the box.

To Richard Furman, my uncle and Mr. Fix-it to my sons. I will never forget our calling my uncle anytime something needed repair in our home. He could fix anything with a paper clip and some bubble gum. I also remember calling on my uncle when I had a difficult math problem to solve. He was always able to get the right answer, although his process was atypical. He was the original innovative thinker. He could fix things that were unfixable, and invent things unheard of. He is a perfect example of a 21st-century, future-ready person with an innovative mind.

Contents

Foreword xi

INTRODUCTION 1

How the Future-Ready Challenge Works 3
Preparing Today's Students to Become Tomorrow's Leaders 4
Your Digital Age Skills Guide 8
Support for the Challenge 13

THE FUTURE-READY CHALLENGE **PART ONE**
WEEKS 1–9

WEEK 1
IMPLEMENT SOFT SKILLS
INTO YOUR LESSON PLANS 22

Challenge 22
Example 22
Suggestions 23
Reflection 23

WEEK 2
AVOID THE WRDR CYCLE 22

Challenge 27
Example 27
Suggestions 28
Reflection 29

WEEK 3
LIGHTS OUT 31

Challenge 33
Example 33
Suggestions 35
Reflection 35

Contents

WEEK 4
NETWORKING 37
Challenge 38
Example 39
Suggestions 40
Reflection 41

WEEK 5
TRANSCEND THE CLASSROOM WALLS 43
Challenge 44
Example 44
Suggestions 46
Reflection 46

WEEK 6
START A PROJECT 47
Challenge 48
Example 48
Suggestions 50
Reflection 50

WEEK 7
THE DEBATE 51
Challenge 53
Example 53
Suggestions 54
Reflection 54

WEEK 8
TOSS OUT THE TEXTBOOK 57
Challenge 59
Example 59
Suggestions 60
Reflection 61

WEEK 9
DO WHAT YOU DO BEST 63
Challenge... 64
Example 65
Suggestions 65
Reflection.. 65

THE FUTURE-READY CHALLENGE **PART TWO**
WEEKS 10-18

WEEK 10
THE VALUE OF RESEARCH 71
Challenge... 74
Example... 74
Suggestions 76
Reflection 76

WEEK 11
THE ART OF CONSTRUCTIVE FEEDBACK 79
Challenge... 81
Example... 81
Suggestions 83
Reflection 83

WEEK 12
LET THEM BE CREATIVE 85
Challenge... 87
Suggestions 87
Reflection 88

WEEK 13
DISCUSS ENTREPRENEURSHIP 89
Challenge... 91
Example... 91
Suggestions 92
Reflection 92

Contents

WEEK 14

DIGITAL CITIZENSHIP 95

What Does Digital Citizenship Encompass? 96

Challenge...100

Example..100

Suggestions 101

Reflection 101

WEEK 15

EMPOWER STUDENT VOICE..105

Challenge...108

Reflection 108

WEEK 16

CREATE STUDENT SCHOLARS..109

Challenge...110

Example..111

Suggestions 112

Reflection 112

WEEK 17

GRADING—THE BIG CHANGE...115

Challenge...117

Reflection 117

WEEK 18

LOOKING TO THE FUTURE..119

Challenge...120

Reflection 121

Conclusion...122

REFERENCES..123

ISTE STANDARDS 125

2016 ISTE Standards for Students 125

Foreword

If you ask a teacher what they really want their students to get out of their class, it's not what's in the textbook. It's communication, collaboration, critical thinking, and the other C's, and all the other letters in the list of 21st-century skills. It is sad and unfortunate, therefore, that what students usually get is what's in the textbook—the names and dates, the math facts and formulas, the punctuation rules. For the most part, they get information, but they don't learn the skills they will need to be successful. It's what my good friend Maria Anderson, in her dissertation on the use of technology in education, called the Knowing-Doing Gap—everybody knew about it, and everybody liked it, but few did anything with it (Anderson, 2009). The desire to teach 21st-century skills is another prime example of the Knowing-Doing Gap.

Fortunately, Rob Furman has provided a bridge across the Gap. Most teachers agree that skills are more important than simply "covering the material," but covering the material is what they do anyway. Why? Because it's familiar; they know how to do it and, for that, they do it pretty well; they don't have to learn a new way, and they don't want to make mistakes. They've been through the learning curve to teach in the traditional way; they don't want to start at the bottom of a new curve.

These are all very good reasons for the existence of the Gap. Teachers are no different from anybody else—from corporate executives, government bureaucrats, and anyone who shies away from taking a risk to learn a new set of skills. It's not easy, it is risky, and you are not very good at it for a while. Nevertheless, we have to do it, once in a while and for a very good reason.

Well, we haven't changed fundamental education in more than 100 years. It's commonly believed that Tom Watson, the founder of IBM as we know it in 1915, would not understand that business today, but Thomas Dewey could walk into most classrooms today and know exactly what is going on. The reason is that students, particularly in secondary and early collegiate education, are not being served by the traditional model. They are exposed to the same material in the same subjects year after year, and never taught or even given the opportunity to practice using that material for relevant ends.

It's time we changed that, and this book is a great first step toward doing that. It's a challenge, and challenges are hard. They are supposed to be. But this book hits the right balance between doing what one knows how to do and learning new things. It's step-by-step and full of great ideas for introducing a new way of teaching and learning into our schools today.

Schools are supposed to be learning institutions. They may be for students, but they are rarely that for faculty and staff. They are "knowing institutions," meaning "We know what to teach and how to teach it, so we do not need to learn anything." Tragic. But I can image teachers in a school working their way through this book together—trying, learning, sharing, and evaluating what they do, until they reach the top of that new learning curve—one that is appropriate for the world of today and tomorrow, not the world of yesterday.

Try it. You'll like it!

Peter Bishop, APF, PhD
Teach the Future (www.teachthefuture.org)

INTRODUCTION

Progress is impossible without change, and those who
cannot change their minds cannot change anything.

—GEORGE BERNARD SHAW

Perusing bookstores and libraries is one of my favorite
pastimes. Often I find myself in strange or unusual parts
of the collection. One day particularly comes to mind
when I found myself in the "Self Help" section. I became very
interested in the vast number of books written on the topics of
how to lose weight, or how to stop smoking, or how to become a
vegan. It occurred to me that many of these books were written
around a "challenge" theme: The author challenges you to follow
certain step-by-step instructions and then guarantees success.

Wow! That sounds so simple. If challenges work as an effective
means to bring about change, perhaps we should apply the same
approach to making meaningful changes in education.

With this step-by-step challenge in mind, I decided to create a
90-day (18-week) challenge designed to change the way we think
about our digital age education.

Why 18 weeks? In 1960, a psychologist by the name of Maxwell
Maltz determined that it takes 28 to 30 days to break a bad habit
(Maltz, 1989). Modern psychologists have now posited that it
takes 28 days to create new patterns in our lives, but it takes 90
days to create new habits.

As I thought about our educational calendar, the 18-week challenge seemed to fall nicely into our two-semester school year.

An 18-week challenge affords you the time needed to implement digital age skills into your curriculum. This challenge incorporates realistic changes that you can follow easily and without performing major reconstruction on your curriculum.

We all know that change can be hard, but when it's broken into easy-to-implement steps, the task becomes not only feasible but effortless! *The Future-Ready Challenge* focuses on changing the classroom, your teaching style, and the related procedures to increase opportunities for your students to engage in—and most importantly, adopt—digital age skills.

This sentiment is mirrored by the Future-Ready initiative of the Office of Educational Technology (part of the Office of the Secretary of Education) (tech.ed.gov/FutureReady), which encourages school superintendents to sign a pledge that they are "committing to foster and lead a culture of digital learning in their district and to share what they have learned with other districts." The Office of Educational Technology provides leadership for transforming education through the power of technology and collaborates with other education offices to support the effective use of technology in learning.

This type of educational reform will allow our children to be the creative, innovative collaborators and communicators we know they are and will need to be! We have the information and the statistics at our fingertips, yet possessing the information and being able to connect the dots, so to speak, are two very different things.

Throughout my career, I have preached the importance of equipping our children with digital age skills to many audiences, and I have watched them nod enthusiastically, agreeing with our nation's need for educational reform. Yet I also had many teachers ask, "What can I do to implement change in my classroom? Where do I begin?"

The Future-Ready Challenge is about breaking the habits that have been ingrained into our educational system for close to 200 years!

How the Future-Ready Challenge Works

Here's how it works: Each week you will focus your efforts on implementing that week's change for an entire week. Along with that week's change, you will be given suggestions and advice for increasing your chances of success with that change, as well as a list of digital age skills you can incorporate into your lesson plan. A progress chart will help you stay on track.

The Future-Ready Challenge is designed to grow exponentially, meaning that you won't abandon the previous week's challenge when working on the current week's challenge. Instead, you will implement all of the challenges you have learned, along with the new challenge. By the end, you will have implemented a semester's worth of changes into your teaching system.

The most effective way of carrying out *The Future-Ready Challenge* is to work through the challenges with a partner or team. You may even take the challenge one step further and use it to create a competition among teams in your building or district. This tactic will help you stay motivated and inspired, and will result in a team-building experience, as well.

If you are undertaking *The Future-Ready Challenge* on your own, www.robfurman.com has discussion and support groups where you can talk with other educators, trade ideas, share your experiences, and become inspired. Let's get started!

Preparing Today's Students to Become Tomorrow's Leaders

There is little doubt that our country needs a complete overhaul of its educational system. We are still following the format developed as a result of the Industrial Revolution! Our school system was deeply influenced by three already-created models: the factory, the prison, and the church. Following the church model, we encouraged a disciplined atmosphere; following the factory model, we taught our children the importance of standing in line and keeping everything uniform; and following the prison format, we taught discipline, compliance, and consistent policies and procedures.

The Committee of Ten was established in 1892 by the National Education Association to establish a standard curriculum. The Committee, composed mainly of educators and chaired by Charles Eliot, the president of Harvard University, made major recommendations reflective of the Industrial Revolution that have shaped our educational system for more than 120 years (Meyer, 1967).

Our society, of course, is worlds beyond the Industrial Revolution, yet our schools remain focused on these antiquated ideals. We are in the age of humanity and creativity, yet we still try to force our students to learn via a cookie-cutter approach that simply doesn't work!

Futurists are now getting into the educational scene because they realize if we don't start making changes now, we are going to start losing the next generation of kids who won't be prepared to meet tomorrow's challenges.

Consider this: Just 10 years ago, we didn't have augmented reality or nanobots. Who knows what technologies will be part of our everyday lives in 5, 10, 15 years? According to *Scientific American* (2015), just a few of the emerging technologies in 2015 alone included fuel-cell vehicles, precise genetic engineering techniques (altering the genetic code of plants in a safer way), neuromorphic technology (computer chips that mimic the human brain), and sense-and-avoid drones. Just think what the next 10 years will bring! Also consider that our first graders will only be in 11th grade in 10 years—not even ready to enter the workforce!

Children equipped with digital age skills will not only effortlessly adapt to our technology-driven world but will also be the leaders of tomorrow's technological breakthroughs—many of which will provide solutions to the most pressing global challenges of our time.

Digital age skills encompass a broad collection of character traits as well as knowledge and skills deemed important for success in today's—and tomorrow's—world (Great Schools Partnership, 2014). Depending on who constructs the list—educators, professors, employers, and so on—these skills may differ. When considering digital age skills, you can begin by asking yourself: What skills will be necessary for today's students to excel in contemporary careers, industries, disciplines, and settings?

One of the most readily recognized models, although it is by no means the final word, is the *Framework for 21st Century Learning,* from the Partnership for 21st Century Skills (a coalition bringing together the business community, education leaders, and policymakers). Opinions always differ regarding what skills are most important and what skills should be implemented into public education. Therefore, 21st-century skills is a concept that will be interpreted and applied in many ways from school to school and state to state.

The Partnership for 21st Century Skills recognizes 21st-century skills as a "set of abilities that students need to develop in order to succeed in the information age." According to the Partnership, these skills include the four "C's": collaboration, creativity, communication, and critical thinking.

These skills, although always important and relevant, take on a new significance in our information-based economy. Today's schools must provide students with the opportunity to:

- Think deeply about issues

- Solve problems creatively

- Work in teams

- Communicate clearly through various media

- Learn ever-changing technologies

- Deal with a flood of information

It's important to understand, states Thoughtful Learning, a developer of K–12 resources, that these ideas are not just anecdotes; a wide array of professional groups and organizations report a need for workers that possess the skills just listed (Thoughtful Learning, 2016).

For example, the American Management Association reports that employers need workers who can solve problems creatively, innovate, communicate, think critically, and collaborate (AMA, 2010), whereas the National Association of Manufacturers reports that the lack of workers possessing these skills are "extremely broad and deep, cutting across industry sectors and impacting more than 80 percent of companies surveyed." The association, referring to this lack of skills as a "human capital performance gap," threatens our nation's ability to compete, "emerging as our nation's most critical business issue" (Association for Career and Technical Education, National Association of State Directors of Career Technical Education Consortium and Partnership for 21st Century Skills, 2010).

Other voices agree:

According to Daniel H. Pink, author of *A Whole New Mind* (2015), we are moving from the Information Age to the Conceptual Age. "The future belongs to a very different kind of person with a different type of mind. … Workers will need to build on the skills of the 20th century by mastering a new and different set of skills in the 21st century."

The World Economic Forum (2015) refers to 21st-century skills as "higher-order" skills, but the concept is the same. "In addition to foundational skills like literacy and numeracy, [workers] need competencies like collaboration, creativity and problem-solving, and character qualities like persistence, curiosity and initiative."

The Global Digital Citizen Foundation says that students need to acquire "transparency-level skills" such as:

- Problem solving

- Creativity

- Analytic thinking

- Collaboration

- Communication

- Ethics, action, and accountability

According to the Foundation, "No pupil in the history of education is quite like today's modern learner. This is a complex, energetic, and tech-savvy individual."

We have no idea what the future holds, but we do know that if we must arm our youth with soft skills (also referred to as higher-order skills) such as the ability to communicate, collaborate, problem solve, and be creative, then we need to begin teaching our children soft skills—skills brought about by the unknown.

Your Digital Age Skills Guide

For purposes of this book, we will identify a group of digital age skills with which to work. Of course, you can add your own skills to the list; as I mentioned earlier, it is a dynamic, ever-changing group of skills, and what is listed often depends on who is creating the list. In other words, a businessperson's idea of future-ready skills will very likely include entrepreneurship, whereas an artist will be the first to say creativity is at the top of the list. Both of these skills are important in their own ways, so there's really no right or wrong list.

With that said, I will use the following list of digital age skills that I think are broad and open-ended enough to hit a large cross-section of people:

- Communication
- Collaboration
- Critical thinking/ problem solving
- Citizenship
- Information literacy

- Leadership

- Digital literacy

- Creativity

- Innovation

Communication

Communication ranges from the personal level, to the business level, and all the way to the global level. If we cannot communicate our findings fluidly, succinctly, and clearly, we are at an immediate disadvantage.

Communication is something that has always been of importance. However, it's the *mode* of communication that's changing for our digital age learners. If we think back to the Industrial Revolution again, the need to communicate wasn't vital, as the factory line worker repeating the same task over and over did not have to communicate his ideas, nor did he feel empowered to do so. In the digital age, the factory mindset is rapidly waning, and our children are expected to communicate their ideas and thoughts with each other using tools such as video conferencing and social media. We've become a global society, communicating with one another through a variety of methods and a variety of styles. Communication has never been more important.

Collaboration

Collaboration is the ability to work on a global scale and the ability to work as a team and understand the benefits of multiple people on a team working for a common goal—not just on a local scale, but on a much grander scale.

The job market of the future will require working in teams. For example, there is an educational technology advocacy group for education that is a prime example of what our future workplaces will look like. The company has just a handful of employees on-site, yet the company's employees, located at different sites across the country, frequently engage in team projects via cloud computing. This type of virtual collaboration will be common-place; therefore, our children must have the ability to collaborate with multiple people in multiple locations.

Critical Thinking/Problem Solving

Critical thinking allows us to devise broader, more creative ways of looking at things. Whereas problem solving relates to a specific task, critical thinking is a visionary process—Here's what I want; how do I get there?

With the rate at which technology is advancing, the *unknown* will become commonplace. Our children must be able to predict what is not yet a reality. For example, just a decade ago, who could have predicted global warming or cyber warfare? Therefore, the learners of today must be the workers of tomorrow who have the ability to think through problems with a critical mind—things we cannot even fathom at the moment.

Citizenship

We need to teach our children in terms of digital and physical citizenship. We need to show them that the internet has become a world of its own, and that we need to respect it as much as we do our physical world. We must live in a way and handle our digital world in a way that is appropriate, both morally and legally.

Citizenship is always changing. Digital citizenship, of course, also continues to change, so digital age learners must understand that their actions in the virtual world can have long-lasting conse-quences. But they also must understand citizenship in general and how our global society influences it. For example, collaborating in a team may mean collaborating with individuals from different countries. Citizenship, with a focus on cultural sensitivity, will be valued more than ever.

Information Literacy

Information literacy is our ability to control the sheer amount of information that is available by deftly identifying it, locating it, evaluating it, and using it to help solve the problem at hand.

Have you ever seen a fire hydrant fully open, gushing water? Now consider this: The amount of information on the internet is like the water coming out of that hydrant. Now consider that the information you want to find is like one droplet in that explosion of water. Information literacy involves managing and finding data in an age where the flow of information is ever-growing and the scale is unprecedented.

Leadership

The qualities of an effective leader have been defined as flexibility, confidence, having good interpersonal skills, being a good communicator, being results-oriented, and so on.

Leadership emphasizes the importance of establishing long-term relationships, which requires individuals who are able to inspire, motivate, and build strategic partnerships to address challenges at every level. Elon Musk is a great example of a visionary who has been able to motivate and inspire others to defy limits on what's possible. The companies he created—SolarCity, Tesla Motors, and SpaceX—are part of his vision to change the world.

In the 21st century, teamwork takes the concept of leadership to a new dimension. The term "followers" has become obsolete because collaborations at nearly every level require all individuals to step up and serve as the leader at some point.

Digital Literacy

Digital literacy refers to our ability to use current and future technologies and to understand what technologies we will use to accomplish which tasks.

The workers of the 21st century must know how to use the technology of today so they can be prepared for the technology of tomorrow. They must know what technology is available, its advantages (and even disadvantages), and how to use it. Once they fall behind on the latest technologies, the learning curve will make it difficult to catch up.

Innovation

Innovation is the ability to think outside the box, to come up with the next big thing. It involves taking the current technology and saying, But what if?

Without innovation, what you see is what you get. With the speed at which technology is moving, we must have the next generation ready to take it to the next level. And without innovative thinkers who can ask, What if? we become stagnant.

Creativity

Creativity is the ability to use all of the building blocks to create something new.

Being creative, being able to think outside the box and color outside the lines, remains so important because it allows us to explore things that aren't typical—a constant theme of the 21st century. Our students must develop creative minds and become innovative thinkers who can take an idea into a team environment and bring it to fruition.

Support for the Challenge

Identifying goals and helping ask the important question, *How do I get there?* will help guide you through this challenge. Here are some resources that can help.

ISTE Standards for Students

The ISTE Standards for Students feature a set of seven characteristics of the digital age learner. These include:

Empowered Learner. I use technology to set goals, work toward achieving them, and demonstrate my learning.

Digital Citizen. I understand the rights, responsibilities, and opportunities of living, learning, and working in an interconnected digital world.

Knowledge Constructor. I critically select, evaluate, and synthesize digital resources into a collection that reflects my learning and builds my knowledge.

Innovative Designer. I solve problems by creating new and imaginative solutions using a variety of digital tools.

Computational Thinker. I solve problems by creating strategies and testing solutions.

Creative Communicator. I communicate effectively and express myself creatively using different tools, styles, formats, and digital media.

Global Collaborator. I strive to broaden my perspective, understand others, and work effectively in teams using digital tools.

The ISTE Standards for Students are designed to keep you on track as you explore new ways to integrate digital age skills into your curriculum. The digital age skills are what you want your students to embrace, while the ISTE Standards for Students are who you want them to become: explorers, creators, and discoverers.

In other words, by adopting and incorporating digital age skills into your curriculum, you are in turn opening the door for an empowered student voice and an effective, student-driven process.

Consider ISTE Standards as you work your way throughout the *Future-Ready Challenge* by asking yourself: What types of digital age learners am I aiming to create? The 2016 ISTE Standards for Students are listed in their entirety at the end of the book.

It's also worth mentioning that there are ISTE standards for teachers and administrators as well that help us model for our students. Learn more at iste.org/standards.

The Importance of Backward Design

I have also designed your challenge using the backward design strategy (Figure 1). The backward design strategy has had a long history in education. Ralph W. Tyler first published the concept in his 1949 work, *Basic Principles of Curriculum and Instruction.* Educators and authors Grant Wiggins and Jay McTighe, though, are often considered to have popularized the concept for the modern era in their book *Understanding by Design* (2005). Backward design is an idea that has stood the test of time.

The traditional way of teaching involves teachers beginning with textbooks and lesson plans and then deciding on their targeted goals and standards. Backward design, however, flips the script, instead encouraging teachers to let the goal drive the curriculum.

Backward design can be thought of as a purposeful task analysis. In other words, when given a task to be accomplished, we ask ourselves: *How do we get there?*

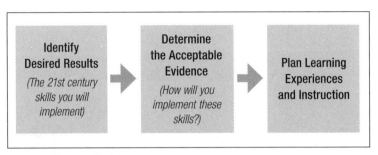

Figure 1 • Backward Design

This type of thinking allows us to depart from thinking about assessment as something we do at the end. So instead of creating assessments at the conclusion of a unit of study, backward design encourages us to operationalize our goals as we begin planning a unit or course of study.

You will practice the backward design theory throughout your 18-week challenge as you consider the digital age skills on which you want to focus and then develop plans for implementing them.

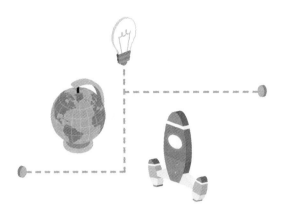

THE FUTURE-READY CHALLENGE
PART ONE

WEEKS 1-9

The future depends on what we do in the present.

— MAHATMA GHANDI

+ + + + +

Congratulations. By choosing this book and deciding to take part in this challenge, you are taking an important step toward improving learning experiences and preparing your students for the future.

The challenges for weeks 1 through 9 share important steps you as an educator can take to embed 21st-century skills into your lessons. Starting at the beginning, with a list of soft skills and a meditation on how to incorporate them into your instruction, the challenges move from conceptualizing to avoiding repetition to focusing on specific outcomes. Case studies and examples provide fodder for inspiration.

Worksheet 1 will help you stay focused and organized. Remember that each challenge is exponential. By Week 9 you should be incorporating the first nine challenges. Check off each challenge as you complete it for that week.

Worksheet 1

Challenge	Week 1	Week 2	Week 3	Week 4	Week 5	Week 6	Week 7	Week 8	Week 9
Implement Soft Skills into Your Lesson Plans									
Avoid the WRDR Cycle									
Lights Out									
Networking									
Transcend the Classroom Walls									
Start a Project									
The Debate									
Toss Out the Textbook									
Do What You Do Best									

WEEK 1

IMPLEMENT SOFT SKILLS INTO YOUR LESSON PLANS

Plans are nothing; planning is everything.

—DWIGHT D. EISENHOWER

To make the *Future-Ready Challenge* a success, you must start at the beginning, in the planning stages, because when changes aren't structured, you can't measure their growth. In other words, you have to know what you're aiming for. And to do this, you must mindfully begin to implement digital age skills into your everyday lessons.

Challenge

Your challenge is to add a line to your lesson plans that includes the digital age skill(s) being developed. Aim to do this for every class you teach, every day you teach. Your awareness of incorporating digital age skills into your everyday lessons is simply the most effective way to impact your students' understanding and learning of these skills. This simple addition to your daily lesson plans will benefit your students for years to come.

Example

Consider creating a lesson where students must collaborate in order to solve a problem. In other words, go beyond memorization and dive into problem solving. Design a problem that includes multiple parts in order to solve the problem or multiple ways to solve the problem.

A great example for the social studies teacher is Countable (countable.us), a government website and app that allows kids to look at active bills in Congress and choose a position. You choose an active bill and ask the students to debate whether the bill should be passed or opposed. Encourage them to choose a position, research it, and present their argument to the class. Using the Countable app, allow the students to write directly to their congressperson.

This is, by far, one of the most important weeks in the challenge, as you will begin building an awareness of digital age skills and ISTE standards and how implementing these standards will bring about positive change.

FUTURE-READY **DETAILS**

--●

Digital Age Skills Used	ISTE Standards Addressed
• Innovation	• Global Collaborator
• Creativity	• Empowered Learner
• Communication	• Digital Citizen
• Collaboration	• Creative Communicator
• Digital Literacy	
• Critical Thinking/ Problem Solving	

Remember: The digital age skills you use will be what you want your students to adopt, and the ISTE standards are who you want your students to become.

Suggestions

Create a spot in your lesson plan where you can physically write down the digital age skills you will be touching on. You can then refer to these skills as you write out your lesson plan, even marking the areas in the lesson plan where each skill will be incorporated.

Reflection

After completing this challenge, ask yourself the following questions. This is an excellent opportunity to share with a peer who is undertaking the challenge as well.

1. In what ways did this challenge change/influence my teaching style? How have my students and I benefited from this change?

2. In what ways did the challenge change the way my classroom functions? How did this improve the learning process?

3. How did the use of technology and digital resources facilitate the implementation of this challenge in my classroom? Which resources were the most effective? How can I use these resources to further develop and advance my curriculum?

WEEK 2

AVOID THE WRDR CYCLE

The only way to make sense out of change
is to plunge into it, move with it, and join the dance.

—ALAN WATTS

y wife and I hate to do laundry. It's a never-ending, endlessly repeating process. You know even while you are doing it that you will have to do it again tomorrow. You just go through the motions, not paying much attention to what you are doing. What we don't want to do to our kids is repeat that same monotonous, pointless cycle in the classroom. We don't want our kids to come to school thinking that today will be just like yesterday.

We're all guilty of it at some time or another: just going through the motions. It's time to say goodbye to the days of the packet professor—the teacher who hands off worksheets to the kids when they come in and then proceeds to check out. We continue to have digital age packet professors; those teachers who hand their students an iPad and tell them to work on an app for the next 40 minutes. We may have digitized the process, but it's really no different. I call it the Wash, Rinse, Dry, Repeat (WRDR) cycle, and many of us are caught in it.

If your students can always anticipate the classroom structure, you may be a WRDR teacher! You know the routine: a worksheet bell ringer, followed by a review of last night's worksheet/ homework, followed by opening up the book and working on another worksheet, and so on, and on. Each day is identical to the next. Does it fit the lesson plan structure? Yes. Does it fulfill the minimum requirements? Probably. Is it quality teaching? Absolutely, 100 percent *no!*

The WRDR cycle is indicative of the Industrial Revolution mentality, and it is a cycle we must break. Our students will never be in a system where they will earn money doing a job that is as cyclical as in the days of the factory. Therefore, we are doing them an injustice by teaching them in the same fashion.

Think back to when you were a student: Which lessons were the most memorable to you? I guarantee they were ones where the teacher encouraged you to participate in the learning process in a unique and creative way. I remember a time in fifth grade when we spent the day acting and being treated like children in Colonial times. The wealth of information I learned that day was astronomical because I was actively engaged in the learning process. This is why we must avoid the WRDR cycle.

Challenge

Break the WRDR cycle in your classroom. It's up to you! Keep your mind firmly focused on memorable and engaging project-based learning.

Example

Instead of going through the WRDR cycle, change up your next science lesson and team up with the school's art teacher to engage your students in the creative process:

Elementary School Level

Have a rain gutter regatta! Engage their creativity and allow your students to create mini flotillas. But don't stop there. Take the opportunity to teach them about water density and wind currents, and encourage them to design their boats to maximize wind potential.

Middle School Level

The lesson is on circuits. Head to your local junk store and buy a broken electric guitar. Gut it and start over. Your students will design a new guitar body based on acoustic concepts. Engage their artistic abilities by asking the art teacher to discuss the ways they can decorate the guitar. In the meantime, organize your students into teams and give each team a project—rebuilding the ground wire, the switch between pickups, the volume control, the cable from the guitar to the amp, and so on. How does a ground wire work? How does sound travel? What are the concepts of circuitry, electricity, tension, and acoustics?

High School Level

Your students will create their own business plan. Bring in experts from local businesses and set up a Shark Tank style game. Your students will create a product and a business model, and the "sharks" will judge them.

FUTURE-READY **DETAILS**

Digital Age Skills Used

- Creativity
- Communication
- Collaboration
- Critical Thinking/ Problem Solving
- Leadership

ISTE Standards Addressed

- Empowered Learner
- Knowledge Constructor

Suggestions

Keep the following things in mind as you work through this challenge:

1. Don't be afraid to take a risk! Just try something.

2. If it's boring to you, chances are it's boring to them. Put yourself in their shoes and ask yourself: If I were a student, would I find this interesting?

3. If you can predict what your class will look like two months from now, you are a WRDR teacher!

4. If it sounds like a crazy, weird lesson, it probably is, and that's okay—your students will never forget it!

Reflection

Ask yourself these questions at the end of Week 2.

1. In what ways did this challenge change/influence my teaching style? How have my students and I benefited from this change?

2. In what ways did the challenge change the way my classroom functions? How did this improve the learning process?

3. How did the use of technology and digital resources facilitate the implementation of this challenge in my classroom? Which resources were the most effective? How can I use these resources to further develop and advance my curriculum?

TOOHAK!

While teaching a seventh grade World Cultures course in my first year, I discovered a tremendous website that engages all students in reviewing for upcoming assessments. It's called Kahoot! While preparing questions for each unit, I found myself digging through my notes packets, textbook information, and study guides to create questions for my students.

As I did this, I came to the realization that my own knowledge of the course content grew as I was typing the questions and answer choices. With access to a 1:1 student-to-computer ratio, I decided to flip things around and create a backwards version of the game. Instead of my creating the review questions, my students set up Kahoot! accounts, and *they* make the questions.

When they are finished, they share their link and have their classmates and even myself play their game. It's called TOOHAK!—the backwards version of Kahoot!

Matthew J. Jones, 7th Grade World Cultures Teacher
South Park Middle School, South Park School District
South Park, Pennsylvania

+++++

WEEK 3

LIGHTS OUT

You can't stop a teacher when they want
to do something. They just do it.

— J.D. SALINGER

A s teachers, we are suffering from an overload
of content because our educational system
seems to never let go of anything old; instead,
it is always adding new things to the curriculum. For
example, in some countries, third graders are asked
to use just a handful of content themes, whereas we
are in the hundreds!

Here's my thought: We are trying to teach more than is necessary! We are currently engaged in the "mile wide, inch deep" curriculum. We must begin selectively discarding—turning off the lights—on content that just isn't realistic, useful, or worthwhile anymore.

I like to think of it as "Lights Out" on waste. Another way to think about this concept has been termed "curriculum compacting." The result is the same. We need to make room for in-depth learning.

For example, is teaching cursive writing really a necessary area of study anymore? How much time do our elementary school teachers spend teaching cursive writing? Couldn't that time be spent learning ideas that are far more relevant?

Early childhood expert Laura Dineheart and the founder of the website handwritingrepair.com, Kate Gladstone, both agree that there is a place for handwriting in the very early years, but holding on to cursive education is akin to holding on to calligraphy. Cursive writing has become more of a cultural tradition than a necessary skill. This is the age of iPads, cell phones, and computers. We need to focus our teaching on computer-based communication. Cursive? Lights Out!

Other examples include spelling, memorization of math facts, and dates. If the truth be known, spelling has been taught in the same manner for a hundred years: Introduce words on Monday. Write sentences on Tuesday. Write words 10 times each on Wednesday. Play spelling games on Thursday, and test on Friday. Does that sound like digital age skill development? Wouldn't it make more sense to teach spelling as a part of communication skills? Lights Out!

Memorizing math facts is certainly a necessary skill for our students. Math facts should be an automatic response to all math problems, but let's consider using technology to support this skill development while it is being mastered. Instead of math fact times drills, let's use math facts to solve problems. Lights Out!

Memorizing battles and dates just has to be a thing of the past. We ask Siri for any arbitrary information with instant satisfaction. Lights Out!

The idea of "lights out" doesn't necessarily mean eliminating one concept and not looking back. It means prioritizing our time differently and thinking beyond the tip of our noses. For example, it doesn't necessarily mean eliminating handwriting from our curriculum; it may mean making it less of an emphasis so as to allow other content themes to take a front seat.

Challenge

Throw some things away! Turn out the lights on content that is no longer applicable because of our current and future technologies. Find ways to spend your—and your students'—time more productively and more appropriately for what they will need to know in the future. Think in terms of concept-driven ideas.

Example

Elementary School Level

Instead of countless lessons on handwriting, pass it off to the art teacher for a lesson in calligraphy! Calligraphy is an art form that allows students to concentrate on the strokes of a letter.

The benefits of learning letters and handwriting are still there, but making it an art assignment will free up additional time throughout your day.

Middle School Level

You are teaching a lesson on the Civil War. Instead of requiring your students to memorize the dates, places, and so on associated with this war, turn your attention to military strategy—important for both critical thinking and problem solving. Have a debate about Lee's and Grant's strategies during the Civil War and how they shaped the outcome of the war. Encourage your students to take sides and plan a strategy, taking into consideration everything about their military strategy, including food and supplies.

You can also encourage creative thought by creating an alternative history assignment. Ask them how the outcome could have changed if aerial bombing or automatic weapons were used? How may have that changed the United States? Encourage your students to collaborate in groups and brainstorm ideas. Ask them to consider how our country could be different had the South won the war. Take it one step further and talk with a classroom across the country or across the globe about how the world would view the United States in this alternate reality.

High School Level

Instead of a typing class, have the students work in voice-activated systems. Go one step further and encourage them to brainstorm ideas on what they think will be the next form of nonverbal communication.

FUTURE-READY DETAILS

Digital Age Skills Used	ISTE Standards Addressed
• Collaboration	• Global Collaborator
• Innovation	• Empowered Learner
• Communication	• Innovative Designer
• Critical Thinking/ Problem Solving	• Computational Thinker
	• Creative Communicator

Suggestions

Do the right thing even though no one is watching! This may mean doing what's right for your students, regardless of bureaucracy.

Take the time to carefully examine your curriculum and find content that isn't relevant anymore because of current and future technologies. This curriculum should be eliminated or compacted.

Increase the use of project-based learning to put digital age skills at the forefront.

Reflection

Congratulations! You now have three challenges under your belt. Keep the momentum going and reflect on what you have learned by asking the following questions.

1. In what ways did this challenge change/influence my teaching style? How have my students and I benefited from this change?

2. In what ways did the challenge change the way my classroom functions? How did this improve the learning process?

3. How did the use of technology and digital resources facilitate the implementation of this challenge in my classroom? Which resources were the most effective? How can I use these resources to further develop and advance my curriculum?

NETWORKING

Alone we can do so little;
together we can do so much.

— HELEN KELLER

ith our ability to communicate so easily on a global scale, we should be learning from other experts in the field on a regular basis. Just as our students should no longer rely on their teachers to be the sole keeper of content, neither should we be learning solely through school-based professional development. We need to reach out on our own and network with other educators, using the internet and social media platforms to our advantage.

There are countless teachers doing great things, so why shouldn't we share what they've learned? And why shouldn't we share our own knowledge and our experiences with others? Teachers networking with other teachers raises the professional bar in education and makes us all better teachers.

As educators, we must practice what we preach. Modeling is important! If we want our students to understand the value of networking, then we need to be part of it. We can use the power of networking to learn amazing things and to model it for our students. The internet has so much information. Through networking, we can access it, attack it, and use it.

Challenge

Share your knowledge and experiences with your colleagues, and take the time to learn from theirs.

Pinterest (pinterest.com) is a fantastic place where teachers gather to share content. I even did a half-day professional development program on Pinterest with my teachers! During this program, the teachers created their own boards, and then we created a board to share. Now my teachers are sharing with each other around the clock. It's not just a professional development day—it's all day, every day!

Twitter is another remarkable social platform that allows teachers to have meaningful conversations with their peers and with experts around the globe.

Blogs have also become a valuable outlet for educators who want to share their content and learn from their colleagues' content. Some of my favorites include:

- Edutopia: edutopia.org

- International Society for Technology in Education (ISTE): iste.org

- Association for Supervision and Curriculum Development (ASCD): ascd.org

- LinkedIn: linkedin.com

- Goodreads: goodreads.com

Example

Elementary School Level

The website ePals (epals.com) was one of the first to engage in the electronic pen pal idea. ePals allows students to work with other students from other locations, building bonds and friendships and working on critical skills and thinking experiences. ePals allows your students to collaborate with classrooms around the world. For example, read a story about the Revolutionary War and create an ePals experience with a classroom from England.

Middle School Level

Encourage your students to network with authors and experts to generate ideas.

High School Level

Encourage your high school students not only to find networks to communicate with others but also to create their own networks, allowing them to become experts and help future students benefit from their knowledge.

FUTURE-READY **DETAILS**

--●

Digital Age Skills Used

- Collaboration
- Critical Thinking/ Problem Solving
- Communication
- Innovation
- Digital literacy

ISTE Standards Addressed

- Global Collaborator
- Creative Communicator
- Creative Designer
- Digital Citizen

Suggestions

Begin by finding just one social media outlet where you feel comfortable. Within that platform, find a few like-minded educators in that realm.

Don't reinvent the wheel if you are looking for digital age content to incorporate into your curriculum. Look for other educators who have already done that and use their experience as inspiration.

Don't hesitate to share your ideas. Networking allows you to reap the benefits from others' content, but you must also have the willingness to share and add to the information available to educators.

Reflection

This week's challenge is a great opportunity to network with your peers. Answer the following questions for yourself and then compare with someone else.

1. In what ways did this challenge change/influence my teaching style? How have my students and I benefited from this change?

2. In what ways did the challenge change the way my classroom functions? How did this improve the learning process?

3. How did the use of technology and digital resources facilitate the implementation of this challenge in my classroom? Which resources were the most effective? How can I use these resources to further develop and advance my curriculum?

TRANSCEND THE CLASSROOM WALLS

The art of teaching is the art of assisting discovery.

— MARK VAN DOREN

hen we examine some of the companies considered to be on the cutting edge of the 21st century (Google, Apple, etc.), it becomes quickly apparent that our nation doesn't work in four-walled rooms anymore. Once again we are reminded that we are far removed from the days of the factory with four walls and an assembly line. Instead, many of today's companies feature large, warehouse-style settings where cubicles are non-existent, where bean bags replace chairs, and where centrally located television screens facilitate communication with colleagues from around the world.

This new way of working means that we must prepare our students to be globally aware and globally interactive. Working on business projects with colleagues from around the world will be commonplace. Video chats and virtual reality worlds will be their norm. As educators, we want our students to experience learning without the confines of the classroom walls.

The NEA states that our workforce skills and demands have changed dramatically in the past 20 years. The rapid decline in "routine" work has been well documented by many researchers and organizations. At the same time, there has been a rapid increase in jobs involving nonroutine, analytic, and interactive communication skills. Today's job market requires competencies such as critical thinking and the ability to interact with people from many linguistic and cultural backgrounds (cultural competency).—National Education Association, *Preparing 21st Century Students for a Global Society*

Challenge

Transcend the classroom walls and allow your students to engage with other students from across town, across the nation, or across the world. There are so many great ways to bring the world to your students.

Example

Elementary School Level

Mystery Skype. Mystery Skype is a challenge that involves your classroom and another classroom somewhere else in the world. It is your students' goal to guess the location of the other school before they guess yours by asking only yes or no questions.

Skype and Author Network. Skype and Author Network allows your students to connect with a children's book author via Skype. It's a great opportunity for your children to have a conversation with a favorite author!

Middle School Level

At the middle school level, students can consider a product that would be a valuable addition to a community. They can then locate local experts who can help them make their idea come to fruition.

High School Level

Create shadow experiences for your students that allow them to work alongside professionals in a specific profession or industry. Take it one step further and allow your students to take their research-backed ideas to businesses.

FUTURE-READY **DETAILS**

---●

Digital Age Skills Used

- Collaboration
- Creativity
- Communication
- Digital Literacy
- Critical Thinking/ Problem Solving

ISTE Standards Addressed

- Global Collaborator
- Empowered Learner
- Innovative Designer
- Creative Communicator

Suggestions

Start simple! Attempting to Skype with another classroom in China may prove to be challenging for your first project. Instead, connect with an educator across town and practice Skyping with that classroom for a fun experience.

Reflection

You are making great progress through the Future-Ready Challenge and are likely making some interesting observations as well. Be sure to write them down along with your answers to the following questions.

1. In what ways did this challenge change/influence my teaching style? How have my students and I benefited from this change?

2. In what ways did the challenge change the way my classroom functions? How did this improve the learning process?

3. How did the use of technology and digital resources facilitate the implementation of this challenge in my classroom? Which resources were the most effective? How can I use these resources to further develop and advance my curriculum?

WEEK 6

START A PROJECT

Project-based learning: Learning about different subjects simultaneously by guiding students through a real-world problem, develop a solution using evidence to support a claim, and presenting a solution through a multimedia approach based on 21st century tools.

—EDUTOPIA (EDUTOPIA.ORG)

You know the drill: Textbook in hand, you start going page by page, chapter by chapter, worksheet by worksheet—until you are bored stiff. Frankly, if you are bored, I guarantee your students are, too!

Think about your education as a child. Do you remember a project you worked on, or a paper you completed? I guarantee you it's the project! Let your students work on projects and make discoveries for a meaningful experience. Project-based learning in the 21st century is more important than ever because there are so many new things being discovered all the time.

A project doesn't have to be a large undertaking; it can be a single lesson, so don't think of project-based learning as something difficult to incorporate into your curriculum. Project-based learning engages your students, sparks their creativity, and allows you to incorporate any number of digital age skills into one project. There's always more learning going on within a 30-minute project than a 30-minute lecture.

Remember: Project-based learning experiences allow your students to learn the information as they create something. It's not something that's done after your students have learned the information; it's something that's done while your students are learning. It's part of the learning process!

Challenge

Create a project-based learning experience that meets the standards you are working to implement.

Example

Elementary School Level

Teach your students about grammar, sentence structure, and plot design by creating a story project. As their stories take shape, you will find plenty of opportunities to teach these concepts.

Middle School Level

Consider a physics class where you want to teach your students the physics involved in structuring a bridge. Sure, you could show a video of a bridge being built and discuss weights and balances. But wouldn't it be far more advantageous to engage your students by allowing them to build their own miniature bridge? Encourage them to collaborate as a team and research the best bridge design, the physics of the structure, and the math problems to back up their ideas. The bridge project not only teaches your students the standards of physics but also encourages them to become self-directed learners.

High School Level

Your students will create a 5K race that attempts to understand how elevation and incline (both up and down) affect speed. After designing the race's route (or multiple routes), they will run it and test their results.

FUTURE-READY DETAILS

Digital Age Skills Used	ISTE Standards Addressed
• Critical Thinking/ Problem Solving	• Global Collaborator
• Communication	• Empowered Learner
• Collaboration	• Knowledge Constructor
• Innovation	• Innovative Designer
• Digital literacy	• Creative Communicator

Suggestions

Make an effort to introduce one project each nine weeks.

Pick a more mundane theme or topic and find a way to make it more interesting for your students by introducing a project.

Make your project worthwhile by touching on a number of standards. Be able to identify the standards you want to convey to your students.

Reflection

1. In what ways did this challenge change/influence my teaching style? How have my students and I benefited from this change?

2. In what ways did the challenge change the way my classroom functions? How did this improve the learning process?

3. How did the use of technology and digital resources facilitate the implementation of this challenge in my classroom? Which resources were the most effective? How can I use these resources to further develop and advance my curriculum?

WEEK 7

THE DEBATE

For good ideas and true innovation, you need
human interaction, conflict, argument, debate.

—MARGARET HEFFERNAN

I have learned over the years that the adults in our
society seem to have difficulty disagreeing with
each other without attacking one another and
going for the jugular. I believe many of us lack the
ability to effectively debate simply because of a lack
of positive debating experiences in school.

In order for our students to succeed in the digital age, we need to teach them how to find a topic, research that topic, form an opinion based on that research, and be able to defend their opinion—not with personal attacks or negativity; just intellect based on research.

Create a supportive environment where your students can experience constructive criticism in a positive way. Use the debate platform as an opportunity to teach them the power of positive debate. Allow them to be risk takers in a nonthreatening environment.

DEBATE RESOURCES

Need help getting started and modeling a positive debate platform? These sites offer inspiration and advice for introducing the art of the debate to your students:

The International Debate Education Association (idebate.org) has a plethora of teacher resources that will motivate and inspire you.

The Noisy Classroom (noisyclassroom.com) is dedicated to promoting and supporting the use of speaking and listening in the classroom. The site offers strategies, ideas, and lesson plans to get your started.

The Teaching Channel (teachingchannel.org) has short videos that show you how to encourage your students to share and respond to one another:

teachingchannel.org/videos/encourage-student-debate-getty

teachingchannel.org/videos/evaluating-both-sides-of-argument

teachingchannel.org/videos/evidence-arguments-lesson-planning

A supportive, nonthreatening environment is one in which you teach your students how to disagree and how to argue with purpose. They will quickly learn that they must research their opinions and use facts to have a lively debate. A positive debating experience creates an atmosphere that allows students to research and communicate their ideas. This type of experience teaches students that to win a debate, they must play by the rules.

Positive debating experiences provide all students—even those with less confidence—a safe haven that allows them to share their ideas.

Challenge

Teach your students to argue and defend a topic.

Example

A great way to introduce debate to your students is through the Countable app (countable.us), which shows all active bills in Congress. Your students can read about these bills, choose one, and form an opinion. Consider splitting your class in half and assigning each side the yea or nay. Then ask each side to research the bill and defend it based on their research. After the debate, take a vote and send the class's decision to the Countable app.

The bill you choose will depend on the grade level of your students. For example, at the elementary school level, your students may debate a bill on whether the United States should go back to the moon, while at the middle school level, your students may debate a bill on whether we should allow inmates to vote. At the high school level, your students can tackle bills involving hot-button topics such as fracking.

FUTURE-READY **DETAILS**

---•

Digital Age Skills Used	ISTE Standards Addressed
• Collaboration	• Global Collaboration
• Digital Literacy	• Empowered Learner
• Communication	• Knowledge Constructor
	• Creative Communicator

Suggestions

Use the Countable app for any subject, any grade level. It provides an instant debate platform. The Countable app is ideal because any teacher can use it! Math teachers can find a bill related to economics, while music teachers can find a bill related to the arts.

PBS has an excellent resource (watchthedebate.org) that has every presidential debate video since 1960. You can use this site to browse debates, find highlights, track how candidates debate specific issues, and teach your students debating strategies.

Reflection

Reflect on how undertaking the debate challenge affected your teaching and your students' learning. You might consider the following:

1. In what ways did this challenge change/influence my teaching style? How have my students and I benefited from this change?

2. In what ways did the challenge change the way my classroom functions? How did this improve the learning process?

3. How did the use of technology and digital resources facilitate the implementation of this challenge in my classroom? Which resources were the most effective? How can I use these resources to further develop and advance my curriculum?

CASE STUDY   +++

Solving the Mysteries of Our Past

One of my favorite project-based learning experiences involves the concept of meaningful debate. During the unit on drawing conclusions, I present my students with a real-life investigation inspired by the television series *History Detectives*.

The project begins with the students watching a short clip of the video. They record all of the given facts and discuss the information that they still need to know in order to confidently arrive at a conclusion.

Throughout this experience, students work collaboratively in groups and read nonfiction texts to collect further information, compare and contrast their findings, and confidently choose a stance on the mystery at hand.

As students begin to formulate their opinions based on their research findings, they are challenged to consider the opposing side's stance and refute the evidence that the opposing side obtained to support their conclusion.

Continued

Debating is an authentic exercise that teaches students how to apply text evidence to solve real-world problems and acknowledge the differing views and opinions of others. To fortify their arguments before the actual debate, students often take it upon themselves to seek out additional resources beyond the materials provided by the teacher.

Giving students a purpose for research and a more meaningful evaluative assessment intrinsically motivates them to further their learning beyond expectations. Debating sparks discussion within the classroom, pushing students to think critically about the matter at hand, and requiring them to communicate respectfully with peers who hold opposing views. Skills gained through debating are applicable both within and outside of the classroom.

Beth Poluszejko, 5th Grade Language Arts
South Fayette Intermediate School, South Fayette Township School District
McDonald, Pennsylvania

+++++

WEEK 8

TOSS OUT THE TEXTBOOK

It is the supreme art of the teacher to awaken
joy in creative expression and knowledge.

—ALBERT EINSTEIN

As we make our way to the halfway point of the *Future-Ready Challenge,* it's time to take on an activity that may prove difficult: I want you to throw out the textbook!

As teachers, we have been trained to believe that we cannot possibly do our jobs without our textbook and teacher's manual in hand. In fact, it's gotten so bad that many teachers plan their curriculum around the table of contents. The textbook was never meant to be anything more than a tool; and as with many ancient tools, there is a better replacement. Many textbooks are filled with facts and figures that we simply don't need anymore—some are even inaccurate!

Consider this: With the increased rate at which our world is acquiring knowledge through scientific discoveries and new technologies, before a textbook can be printed it's already outdated!

By getting rid of the textbook, not only will you be on the road to eliminating the WRDR cycle (Week 2) but you will also be putting an end to the monotonous page turn after page turn.

With the concept you want to teach in mind, create a collaborative activity, a creative project, or an issue to debate—then focus on that concept, and teach! You don't need a textbook to do that.

A successful way to begin this venture is to choose several standards that you want to focus on in your next lesson. Instead of the textbook, find current resources on the internet. You will quickly find that using different technology sources will allow you to provide your students with an increased understanding of the content.

This new type of teaching will feel like you are growing wings! You are giving yourself permission to be a more creative teacher. When you get stuck in the cycle of the textbook, you no longer have the freedom to be a creative teacher. Just because a lesson is found in a book doesn't mean it's the best lesson for your students.

The best lesson for your students will come out of the creative mind of a teacher, so give yourself permission to create lessons that are more exciting, more engaging, and more digital age than you will find in any textbook.

Challenge

Toss out the textbook! Instead, use digital age skills to find activities, content, and other experiences related to your content and knowledge standards.

Example

Elementary School Level

Let's assume your curriculum calls for introducing multiplication. Instead of opening up the textbook, reading the explanation, and handing out a worksheet, toss the textbook aside, gather your students, and head outside. After encouraging your students to gather a pile of leaves, start grouping them together in multiples of 2, 3, 4, and so on. Your outdoor lesson has allowed your students to visualize multiplication through a creative activity they won't soon forget!

Middle School Level

Create an online scavenger hunt. Write questions for your students to answer, find websites that hold the answers, and encourage your students to find the answers through internet searches.

High School Level

Instead of using a textbook, have your students research mathematical equations through Khan Academy (khanacademy.org) and take it one step further by allowing them to create their own video tutorial that explains how to answer specific problems for others. You can also create your own school's version of the Khan Academy by saving the video vignettes for future classes.

FUTURE-READY **DETAILS**

--●

Digital Age Skills Used	ISTE Standards Addressed
• Creativity	• Empowered Learner
• Innovation	• Knowledge Constructor
• Critical Thinking/ Problem Solving	• Innovative Designer

Suggestions

Use your networking skills (Week 4) and social media platforms (Week 5) to find creative activities based on the content you want to teach.

Use the textbook as a resource, but not as your curriculum and not as something you use exclusively.

Let your students' interests guide some of your activities.

Reflection

1. In what ways did this challenge change/influence my teaching style? How have my students and I benefited from this change?

2. In what ways did the challenge change the way my classroom functions? How did this improve the learning process?

3. How did the use of technology and digital resources facilitate the implementation of this challenge in my classroom? Which resources were the most effective? How can I use these resources to further develop and advance my curriculum?

CASE STUDY   +++

Bringing Manatees into the Classroom

As a special education teacher who co-teaches in the general education classrooms and does pull-out reading interventions in grades K–4, I must use a number of teaching strategies to grab my students' attention. This often involves learning beyond the textbook.

One particular example of tossing the textbook occurred during a reading comprehension lesson on the skill of fact or opinion. This lesson involved reading a story on manatees and putting the skills of fact or opinion to use with that story. However, my students live in rural West Virginia and haven't had much exposure to animals living outside of their area, so I knew a textbook just wasn't going to reach them.

Continued

Instead, I found a video on YouTube about manatees called "Dragonfly TV Kids Do Science—Manatees." The students were fascinated with the manatee and, just as I thought, many of them had never seen this mysterious creature before.

After building background knowledge with the video, we talked about fact and opinion. In order to reinforce this concept further, I had the students use iPads to go on the "Fact or Opinion: Reading Comprehension Skill Builders" app by Happy Frog. This app helps students look for key words in identifying whether or not the statement is a fact or opinion.

When the manatee selection and fact or opinion activity was presented to the students, I had them work in pairs to complete the activity to integrate cooperative learning into the lesson.

Laurie Brierton, MS, NBCT, Special Education Teacher
New Manchester Elementary School, Hancock County School District
New Cumberland, West Virginia

WEEK 9

DO WHAT YOU DO BEST

Since we live in an age of innovation, a practical education must prepare a man for work that does not yet exist and cannot yet be clearly defined.

—PETER F. DRUCKER

Congratulations! You are halfway through your Future-Ready Challenge! But you may also be starting to feel the slump—perhaps a little frustrated, or perhaps you are feeling like an island, on your own. This is an important time to take a moment and reflect on why you are doing this. In the words of C. S. Lewis, "Integrity is doing the right thing even when no one is watching."

When you close your classroom door and it's just you and your students, teach them how you know they need to be taught. Is it easier to revert back to the days of the packet professor? Of course. But that's not why we became educators. We did it to make a difference in our students' lives. Don't teach your students the way you were taught; teach them the way they need to learn. Do what you do best—no excuses!

We want to create classrooms that emulate the business world of today, which is why these changes are so important. Our job is to prepare our students for college and for a career, and we certainly don't want them to be shell shocked when they enter the real world. We must provide them with these experiences now to prepare them for what's ahead when they become part of our nation's future workforce.

Stay motivated by networking, finding people who are of like mind, exploring social media, sharing your experiences, and gathering new ideas. Talk with your students to get a feel for their appreciation of the changes you initiated. Go to conferences and find validation by connecting with your peers. Share your experiences, challenge each other, and then celebrate your wins.

The idea is to keep moving in the right direction, boost one another, and keep going. You can do this!

Challenge

Conduct an analysis of your progress from the previous nine weeks.

Example

In order to make the Future-Ready Challenge a success, you must take some time to reflect on what you've learned by asking yourself the following questions and using the insight you glean to your advantage as you move toward the next nine weeks:

Which weeks' topics do you feel had the most impact on your students? How can you continue to implement these changes?

Which weeks' topics were the hardest to implement? How can you overcome these challenges in the future?

Which digital age skills were you already using prior to starting the Future-Ready Challenge? Has the Future-Ready Challenge changed the way you implement these skills?

Suggestions

Use this period of reflection to put more time into a topic that was difficult to implement.

Take this opportunity to share your insights with a fellow teacher. Show off a little! Be proud of the changes you've made!

Reflection

1. In what ways did this challenge change/influence my teaching style? How have my students and I benefited from this change?

2. In what ways did the challenge change the way my classroom functions? How did this improve the learning process?

3. How did the use of technology and digital resources facilitate the implementation of this challenge in my classroom? Which resources were the most effective? How can I use these resources to further develop and advance my curriculum?

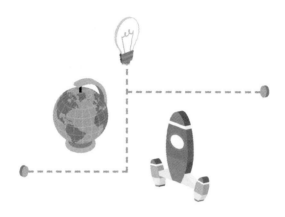

THE FUTURE-READY CHALLENGE
PART TWO

WEEKS 10-18

Develop a passion for learning and you will never cease
to grow.

— ANTHONY J. D'ANGELO

+ + + + +

ou are on the home stretch! Like the first nine weeks, Weeks 10 through 18 are also exponential. However, you must continue to implement the first nine challenges each week. Follow Worksheet 2 for weeks 10 through 18 and remember to continue to use the first nine challenges.

Worksheet 2

Challenge	Week 10	Week 11	Week 12	Week 13	Week 14	Week 15	Week 16	Week 17	Week 18
The Value of Research									
The Art of Constructive Feedback									
Let Them Be Creative									
Discuss Entre-preneurship									
Digital Citizenship									
Empower Student Voice									
Create Student Scholars									
Grading—The Big Change									
Looking to the Future									

WEEK 10

THE VALUE OF RESEARCH

Research is creating new knowledge.

—NEIL ARMSTRONG

C onsider Niagara Falls and the sheer amount of water falling from it. (FYI: It's more than 750,000 gallons per second!) Now consider the existence of one marked droplet of water, and it is your job to locate it! Sounds virtually impossible, doesn't it?

Now consider Niagara Falls as the internet, and the quality information you are looking for is that water droplet somewhere in those falls. Sure, all of the information in the world is available at our fingertips, but do your students possess the capacity to sort through the misinformation, opinions, and downright nonsense to find the quality information they need?

Because of the sheer volume of information on the internet, we need to teach our students to not only research, but research *effectively*. We need to teach students how to research quality content and then how to use that information to form their own opinions and solve their own problems. Without research, and without the knowledge that results from effective research, our 21st-century learners are forced to take in superficial knowledge and opinions from others. And that will always end tragically.

The amazing amount of information available via the internet also means that there is no need to reinvent the wheel! If there's an expert who's already discovered new concepts or new information for which your students are seeking, why would you want to go through the process of finding something someone has already done? In other words, there's a huge advantage to being the curator of the museum—we have the ability to sift through the mountains of information, locate the quality pieces, and create our own solution or opinion based on the research that's already out there. As educators, we must do what we can to impart this knowledge to our digital age learners.

Back in the day, I remember research projects that involved heading to the library, pulling books from the shelves, and writing down research using those small index cards. Of course, we've stopped teaching that method of research because modern methods are easier and more efficient. But in the process, we've also stopped teaching our students the value of locating quality research. Today, we must teach our students how to navigate the waterfall of information that is the internet, locate quality research, and use it properly.

For example, researching Abraham Lincoln can result in everything from conspiracy theories and false claims to peer-reviewed, authentic facts. You want your students to understand the value of official, peer-reviewed literature versus unsubstantiated facts from untrustworthy sources.

RESOURCES FOR EFFECTIVE RESEARCHING

A number of websites will guide you as you teach your students about credible sources, plagiarism, and staying safe online:

Common Sense Media (commonsensemedia.org): Research-based tools allow students to learn the value of technology and lessons allow teachers to guide strategic searches for their students.

Google A Day Challenge (agoogleaday.com): Every day brings a different, challenging question—perfect for allowing your students to hone their research skills.

Teaching Channel (teachingchannel.org): The Teaching Channel features lesson ideas for teaching research skills and videos on how to separate the good sites from not-so-good.

Read Write Think (readwritethink.org): A number of great resources are located here, including a website evaluation form that teaches students how to assess websites.

Google Scholar (scholar.google.com): Google Scholar is a central resource for scholarly articles—ideal for high school students with research experience.

Challenge

Engage your students in a research challenge.

Example

Elementary School Level

Using the website evaluation form from ReadWriteThink (readwritethink.org), encourage your students to explore what makes a website credible. Prepare a set of websites that you can send your students to explore. Then allow them to decide which ones are better used for research and why.

Middle School Level

Your children will create two research papers: one completely written using peer-reviewed and scholarly material, and the other using no peer-reviewed or scholarly sources. This is the perfect lesson to show your students the differences in content and the differences in the resulting research papers!

You might want to use a "spoof" website to get started. These fake sites are used specifically for website evaluation and are a great way to bring home the concept of credibility:

- Tree Octopus (zapatopi.net/treeoctopus)

- Dog Island (thedogisland.com)

- Dehydrated Water (buydehydratedwater.com)

- Save the Rennets (savetherennets.com)

High School Level

This is the level at which you will be encouraging your students to create comprehensive papers based on accurate research. Create a contemporary topic of study and allow them to form an opinion and back up their claims using only accurate research.

Need inspiration? The following sites maintain a list of contemporary topics:

- The Library of Congress, legal topics (loc.gov/law/help/current-topics.php)

- American Psychological Association, psychology topics (apa.org/topics/)

- Real Clear Policy, social issues (realclearpolicy.com/topic/in_the_news/social_issues/)

FUTURE-READY **DETAILS**

Digital Age Skills Used

- Critical Thinking/ Problem Solving
- Digital Literacy
- Information Literacy

ISTE Standards Addressed

- Empowered Learner
- Digital Learner
- Knowledge Constructor

Suggestions

Teach your students the value of using notable, peer-reviewed research engines to eliminate false facts.

Think about predesigning your students' research efforts so that you have an idea what they will find during the research process. Remember: You have to teach research skills before they can begin researching!

After you teach your students how to research, hold them accountable for facts as opposed to opinions.

Reflection

1. In what ways did this challenge change/influence my teaching style? How have my students and I benefited from this change?

2. In what ways did the challenge change the way my classroom functions? How did this improve the learning process?

3. How did the use of technology and digital resources facilitate the implementation of this challenge in my classroom? Which resources were the most effective? How can I use these resources to further develop and advance my curriculum?

Trout in the Classroom

Last year I was able to introduce a truly unique learning experience to my class: Trout in the Classroom, which allowed my students to explore the Pennsylvania state fish, the brook trout. I received a Public Education Leadership Community (PELC) Grant through the PPG Foundation for the aquarium materials. The PA Fish and Boat Commission supplied the trout eggs.

Before the trout arrived, the students viewed a YouTube video that researched promised practices in other Trout in the Classroom schools and piqued their interest. Once the trout arrived, the students engaged in an initial webquest to explore concepts such as the trout life cycle, habitat, and the funnel effect.

Online searches using Google Scholar were an integral component in those lessons. Their searches allowed the students to learn the steps they needed to take to ensure a healthy habitat for the trout.

The students also used technological resources to chart and graph the trout growth, food consumption, and water quality. When fluctuations occurred, such as a decrease in the number of surviving trout, students used problem-solving tactics to figure out what was amiss, and they adjusted the variables like the water temperature, water quality, and food. During this time, my young scholars wrote in journals, reflecting on the trout changes and drawing sketches with labels. In the meantime, I was also able to monitor trends with trout from the same brood by visiting blogs and online chat groups of other Trout in the Classroom (TIC) participants.

Continued

My students also used different modes of technology to peer teach the other third grade classes about the trout. They displayed a class video that recounted the growth of the trout from the hatchery to the classroom. As the video played, the students narrated.

Amy Cramer, Third Grade Mathematics and Science Teacher
South Park Elementary Center, South Park School District
South Park, Pennsylvania

NOTE: Mrs. Cramer's classroom's participation in the Trout In the Classroom program was made possible through a unique partnership between PA Fish and Boat Commission and PA Council of Trout Unlimited. This partnership, coupled with assistance from local conservation organizations, was created to introduce Pennsylvania students to cold water resources and their importance to all communities. The partnership also provides brook trout eggs, trout food, technical assistance, curriculum connections and teacher workshops each year.

WEEK 11

THE ART OF
CONSTRUCTIVE FEEDBACK

Criticism, like rain, should be gentle enough to
nourish a man's growth without destroying his roots.

—FRANK HOWARD CLARK

O ur digital age learners must be able to critique
and be critiqued. And we must give them
the opportunity to create and then give and
receive criticism in a constructive and effective
manner. We need to teach them that there is a
difference between commenting in a negative
fashion and providing constructive criticism.

What I have found is that we are a society of the easily offended. We can't seem to constructively criticize one another without someone being upset. In many cases, we aren't even encouraged to criticize one another in a constructive manner! As digital age learners, our students will need to collaborate effectively to solve problems and create solutions. And to do so, they must be able to take and receive constructive criticism.

It is therefore our job as educators to help our students to provide one another with constructive criticism. And there's no better way to do so then through real-life examples.

The International Literacy Foundation (www.readwritethink.org) refers to this process as peer review, referring to the "many ways in which students can share their creative work with peers for constructive feedback and then use this feedback to revise and improve their work."

The International Literacy Foundation provides a number of helpful strategies for kick starting your constructive criticism project. Their handout, *Peer Edit with Perfection* (IRA/NCTE, 2004), identifies three steps to good peer editing: Compliments, Suggestions, and Corrections. Teach students to use these three steps to give peer feedback.

- Compliment the author: What are a few things you liked about the author's writing?

- Make specific suggestions regarding the author's word choice, use of details, organization, topic, etc.

- Make corrections on the writing piece: Look for spelling, grammar, and punctuation mistakes.

Provide students with sentence starter templates, such as, "My favorite part was _____ because _____," to guide students in offering different types of feedback. After they start with something positive, have students point out areas that could be improved in terms of content, style, voice, and clarity by using another sentence starter: "A suggestion I can offer for improvement is _____."

Teach students what constructive feedback means. Feedback should be done in an analytical, kind way. Model this for students, and ask them to try it. Provide examples of vague feedback versus clear feedback and ask students to point out which kind of feedback is most useful.

For younger students, explain that you need helpers, so you will show them how to be writing teachers for each other. For very young students, encourage them to share personal stories with the class through drawings before gradually writing their own stories.

Create a card and display it in the classroom so students can see the important steps of peer editing. Your steps will vary according to the age of your students.

Challenge

Design a project that will engage your students in the art of constructive criticism.

Example

Elementary School Level

Choose artwork and writing from various third-party sources and guide your students through the process of constructive feedback. Provide them with prompts to get them started. "What I liked best was. ..."

Middle School Level

Have your students write a short story, and publish all of their stories on a blog where they can read each other's stories and leave constructive comments to help improve the story. This allows you to create an online environment where kids can give and receive constructive criticism under your careful watch.

High School Level

The high school level is the ideal time for students to receive feedback not only from their peers, but also from social media and the community at large. The constructive criticism project at this level may involve creating a blog where students will post their work and receive feedback from their classmates. Advertise the blog through social media and encourage feedback from the public. Take the time to critique the feedback from the public with your students, encouraging them to sort through and identify constructive criticism while also helping them manage negative feedback.

FUTURE-READY DETAILS

Digital Age Skills Used

- Communication
- Collaboration
- Critical Thinking/ Problem Solving
- Digital Literacy
- Information Literacy

ISTE Standards Addressed

- Empowered Learner
- Digital Citizen
- Creative Communicator

Suggestions

Remember that you must teach constructive feedback in both directions. You must not only teach your students how to give constructive feedback you must teach them how to accept the feedback in a positive way.

Be a model of constructive feedback in your classroom. Demonstrate to your students that your feedback is helping them work toward a goal.

Reflection

1. In what ways did this challenge change/influence my teaching style? How have my students and I benefited from this change?

2. In what ways did the challenge change the way my classroom functions? How did this improve the learning process?

3. How did the use of technology and digital resources facilitate the implementation of this challenge in my classroom? Which resources were the most effective? How can I use these resources to further develop and advance my curriculum?

CASE STUDY

Game Board Design Challenge

I've implemented a project-based learning unit in math where my students are challenged to engineer an educational game for future students and collaborate with professionals in the educational gaming field. These games target fraction standards that students traditionally find difficult to master.

In the first phase of the project, students work in groups to imagine and design game board concepts that could easily incorporate targeted fraction standards. The students then create a blueprint of their design. Students then have the opportunity to obtain constructive feedback from Francisco Souki, an Advanced Game Board Designer at Schell Games. They use his feedback to determine design modifications.

After creating the game, student designers conduct beta testing by enlisting fifth grade students from other classrooms to play their games. After making multiple changes to their games based on Mr. Souki's feedback and beta testing data, students conduct a final testing phase where a different classroom plays the game and provides constructive feedback through a Google Form.

Students evaluate the games based upon multiple criteria including design, creativity, functionality, and rigor. Based on this feedback, students make final adjustments to their games.

Throughout this process students learn the importance of persistence in achieving a goal when receiving constructive feedback on their work. Students also gain appreciation for the perspectives of others and recognize the value of continuously enhancing their work.

Sarah Manly, Fifth Grade Mathematics Teacher
South Fayette Intermediate School, South Fayette Township School District
McDonald, Pennsylvania

+++++

LET THEM BE CREATIVE

Learning a specific skill set doesn't have the value in today's world that it once did. Learning how to be more creative (and thus adaptable)—now that's what prepares students for life beyond the classroom.

—EDUDEMIC.COM

The idea of being creative gives our communities an opportunity to go beyond what already exists. It is an open-ended concept that knows no boundaries!

Providing our students with an opportunity to be creative will always be a bonus, especially as we prepare our digital age learners for jobs that require global collaboration, communication, and a great deal of creativity. They will be developing things we can't even imagine now! We need creative minds to think of the crazy, outlandish "what-ifs" that become reality. Remember: before it can become fact, it must be fiction.

Our students must have opportunities to be creative and the ability to freely think and explore. The Industrial Revolution didn't require that kind of creativity, but the creative thinkers who can come up with new ideas are the ones who will survive and thrive.

Our digital age learners will be expected to be creative to help their businesses thrive, to help create new products and new information. Without creativity, many of the other digital age skills become less important. For example, without creativity, how are you going to problem solve? How are you going to be able to critically think through ideas? Without using your creative mind, how are you going to collaborate in a team and communicate ideas that may be atypical? Without the ability to be creative, we lose the ability to think about what could happen in the future.

There's no question that we need to give our students an opportunity to be creative. What's great is that any time we take away the world of the worksheet and the packet professor, we have an element of creativity.

So what can we do to help our students flex their creative genius?

In general, the best way to allow our students to be creative is not to give them a process. Give them a room, materials, a concept to build and create—and then get out of their way!

I love concepts like Makerspace (DIY spaces where people can create, invent, and learn), where we can turn our students loose in a room with all sorts of materials and let them create. The idea of being creative should not have boundaries.

As soon as we have boundaries, it becomes managed. The whole idea is to not have rules! We must reject the notion of coloring inside the lines if we are to allow our students' creativity to soar.

There are a number of ways you can spur your students' creativity:

- Consider assigning open-ended projects, which allow students to choose the type of project they want to create. These types of projects allow students to explore their passions. Give them structure with a rubric, but let them guide their discoveries.

- Give your students "genius time," a period of time you devote specifically to allowing your students to explore what interests them. (See Week 16.)

Challenge

Unleash your students' creativity!

Suggestions

Rules create boundaries, which stifle creativity. Don't be afraid to give them something and then walk away.

Don't be specific in how your students should use their creativity. Music, art, a poem? It doesn't matter. Creativity can take many forms!

Give your students the opportunity to take risks when they begin to create. Remind them that risk-taking is always okay.

Creativity does not live in isolation. It can be part of a meaningful assignment or unit of study, and it can also be used as an assessment tool.

Reflection

1. In what ways did this challenge change/influence my teaching style? How have my students and I benefited from this change?

2. In what ways did the challenge change the way my classroom functions? How did this improve the learning process?

3. How did the use of technology and digital resources facilitate the implementation of this challenge in my classroom? Which resources were the most effective? How can I use these resources to further develop and advance my curriculum?

WEEK 13

DISCUSS ENTREPRENEURSHIP

The best way to predict the future is to create it.

—PETER DRUCKER

E ntrepreneurship—it's a concept that's integral to the success of our digital age learners. We need to create students with a business mind who can not only work in a business, but also create one of their own and produce the next big thing. They must be able to answer the question: What does the world need next?

According to a 2012 article in *Forbes*, entrepreneurship concerns the "very engine of economic growth and the people we are counting on—desperately—to rev it up (Nelson, 2012)." Today's students are tomorrow's entrepreneurs, those drivers of economic growth. Entrepreneurship is no longer just a pursuit of the select few.

In other words, it's no longer acceptable to say that only some people are business-minded. We must open up the possibility that our students will enter an entrepreneurial world, and we must be prepared.

Even tomorrow's middle class will be entrepreneurs, creating business, creating jobs, and producing a healthier, more robust economy. Without entrepreneurship we are stagnant! We need students coming out of high school with an understanding of how business works, how to bring ideas to fruition, and a passion for creating.

It's a reality that our students will be far more involved in business than any previous generation. We need to give our students cursory knowledge of those things, because we could very well be teaching the next Mark Zuckerberg! It's our job to open those pathways to them as early as possible. Knowledge of entrepreneurship and how it works will be more important than ever.

As educators, it should be our goal to create experiences for our students that take them through the process of creating products and services. Fortunately, there are a host of ways to set entrepreneurship in motion.

Challenge

Create opportunities for entrepreneurship.

Example

Elementary School Level

Collaborate with the art teacher to allow your students to make arts and crafts that they can sell. Use funny money to let children from other classrooms purchase their classmates' creations.

Middle School Level

Start a school store or improve upon an existing one! Work with your students to determine what products to purchase, order the supplies, and price the supplies. Show them how to reinvest the proceeds back into the store so they can purchase more and better supplies.

High School Level

Your students will work as a group to brainstorm a new product or service, create a product concept and business model, perform market research to determine its need in the marketplace, and even pitch their idea to a local business. Introduce them to Kickstarter (www.kickstarter.com), a unique organization that helps creators find the resources and support needed to turn their ideas into reality.

FUTURE READY **DETAILS**

---●

Digital Age Skills Used

- Communication
- Collaboration
- Critical Thinking/ Problem Solving
- Innovation
- Creativity

ISTE Standards Addressed

- Empowered Learner
- Creative Communicator
- Knowledge Constructor
- Innovative Designer

Suggestions

Avoid discouraging your students because of your personal viewpoint. They could very well have the next great idea!

Consider turning a lesson in entrepreneurship into an opportunity to give back. Explore websites like Causes (www.causes.com), an online platform for discovering, supporting, and organizing fundraising campaigns, and work toward raising money for a cause.

Reflection

1. In what ways did this challenge change/influence my teaching style? How have my students and I benefited from this change?

2. In what ways did the challenge change the way my classroom functions? How did this improve the learning process?

3. How did the use of technology and digital resources facilitate the implementation of this challenge in my classroom? Which resources were the most effective? How can I use these resources to further develop and advance my curriculum?

CASE STUDY

Paws for Tasty Treats Bakery

Students in the life skills classroom at South Fayette Intermediate School have been working on developing their skills as young entrepreneurs. The Paws for Tasty Treats Bakery is a small business where students bake and sell treats to staff members in the building.

Each week the students take orders from teachers for the treat of the week by placing order forms in their mailboxes. On Wednesdays they collect the money and order forms from teachers interested in receiving a treat on Friday. Then they count the money and sort the orders by floor to make for easy delivery on Friday.

This year, teachers are able to create individual bank accounts and withdraw money from their accounts when they would like a tasty treat. The students have to keep track of the money left in accounts and notify teachers when their accounts are running low. After organizing the orders and financials, students get to work reading the recipes, finding and measuring ingredients, and identifying appropriate utensils that need to be used.

After baking, students are responsible for cleanup, putting away materials, and packaging and delivering the treats to teachers.

Continued

In addition to mathematics, reading, and other practical skills that the bakery helps students to master, it also provides practice in the areas of occupational therapy, collaboration, and real-time problem solving. When a problem arises in the bakery, students work with the teacher to find a solution. Because the treats are for sale, they must be tasty and safe for our customers.

The money earned thus far has allowed us to go on additional field trips, purchase utensils, and obtain a full-size refrigerator for the bakery. Looking ahead, we hope to collect all of the recipes we have used thus far and publish them in a cookbook to sell as our next entrepreneurial venture.

Barb Levitt, Life Skills Teacher, Grades 3-5
South Fayette Intermediate School, South Fayette Township School District
McDonald, Pennsylvania

WEEK 14

DIGITAL CITIZENSHIP

Students need to be educated on how to be good citizens of their country and what their rights and responsibilities are as members of society. The same issues need to be addressed with regard to the emerging digital society, so that students can learn how to be responsible and productive members of that society.

—RIBBLE & BAILEY, *DIGITAL CITZENSHIP IN SCHOOLS*

W hat once was science fiction is now a reality. We are living in a society where technology allows us to be in two places at once—a real-life parallel universe! Just as citizenship must be an important part of our students' lives, digital citizenship is a necessity in the cyber universe. In other words, digital citizenship must be as commonplace as physical citizenship.

According to *EdTech Digest,* "Digital citizenship needs to be embraced by educators as a way of thinking—and incorporated, whenever possible, into any type of existing curriculum" (Davis, 2016).

Because our physical presence in the real world is nearly as important as our virtual presence in the cyber universe, a focus on citizenry at both levels is a must for our digital age learners. We want to create good citizens, regardless of whether they are working face to face or in the cyber universe. From posting blogs and images to engaging in group conversations, we want our students to act and behave as they would in the real world.

What Does Digital Citizenship Encompass?

Digital citizenship has been defined many ways, although TeachThought.com arguably articulated it best: "The quality of habits, actions, and consumption patterns that impact the ecology of digital content and communities" (Heick, 2013).

Digital citizenship encompasses a number of topics and themes, often varying based on the age of the child. With younger students, these topics may be as simple as being responsible and respectful while using digital resources. With older students, topics may include everything from understanding digital laws to becoming curators of responsible digital information.

The DC Institute (digitalcitizen.net), a consortium of educators, defines the principles of digital citizenship as:

- Respect yourself and respect others

- Educate yourself and connect with others

- Protect yourself and protect others (Ribble, 2017)

The nine themes of digital citizenship fall under these principles:

You will find that many organizations have created a list of themes within the concept of digital citizenship. The following are among our favorites:

1. **Digital Access.** Working toward equal digital rights and supporting electronic access for everyone

2. **Digital Commerce.** How to be effective consumers in a digital society

3. **Digital Communication.** Making appropriate decisions when faced with many forms of digital communication

4. **Digital Literacy.** Educating people on the importance of information literacy skills

5. **Digital Etiquette.** Understanding appropriate conduct needed to become responsible digital citizens

6. **Digital Law.** Understanding the ethics associated with technology (don't send spam, protect your identity, etc.)

7. **Digital Rights and Responsibilities.** Basic rights afforded to every digital citizen (right to privacy, freedom of speech, etc.)

8. **Digital Health and Wellness.** Understanding physical and psychological well-being in a digital world

9. **Digital Security.** Self-protection in a digital world (virus protection, backup of data, etc.)

Common Sense Media (commonsensemedia.org) focuses on eight topic areas related to digital citizenship:

1. Internet Safety

2. Privacy and Security

3. Relationships and Communication

4. Cyberbullying and Digital Drama

5. Digital Footprint and Reputation

6. Self-Image and Identity

7. Information Literacy

8. Creative Credit and Copyright

In their book, *Digital Citizenship in Schools* (ISTE, 2007), Mike Ribble and Gerald Bailey organized the themes of digital citizenship under Respect, Educate, and Protect:

Respect

- Digital access

- Digital etiquette

- Digital law

Educate

- Digital communications

- Digital literacy

- Digital commerce

Protect

- Digital rights and responsibilities

- Digital safety and security

- Digital health and wellness

Challenge

Help your students grasp the concept of digital citizenship and create an experience where they can demonstrate what it means to be a good digital citizen.

DIGITAL CITIZENSHIP RESOURCES FOR EDUCATORS

Common Sense Media (commonsensemedia.org/educators/training): The Digital Citizenship Curriculum is a one-hour tutorial designed to give educators an introduction to digital citizenship and the many resources (tutorials, webinars, videos, etc.) available through Common Sense Media's Digital Citizenship Curriculum.

iKeepSafe (ikeepsafe.org): iKeepSafe and Google teamed up to provide an interactive, digital-literacy curriculum for teachers of middle and high school students. Some of the features include lessons that help students find reliable online information, stay safe online, recognize bogus information such as fake news and scams, and remain responsible digital citizens.

CyberWise (www.cyberwise.org/educators): CyberWise is a resource for online safety, digital citizenship, privacy, and reputation management. It's also a great site for teachers, offering everything from learning hubs that offer a quick education on some of the biggest concerns related to digital citizenship to online courses, workshops, and the Cyber Civics curriculum, a digital citizenship and literacy curriculum for middle school students.

Digizen (www.digizen.org): Digizen is packed with resources for students, parents, and educators about digital citizenship and what it means to be responsible digital citizens. Their games, videos, lesson plans, and role playing scenarios serve as useful tools for educators introducing digital citizenship to their students.

Example

Elementary School Level

At this stage, it is important to teach physical citizenship and digital citizenship side by side. Your goal is to show students the parallels between the two through role-playing scenarios. Create scenarios that pose the question: What does it mean to be a good citizen? What does it mean to be a good digital citizen? For example, in the physical world, being a good citizen for children means reaching out to a trusted adult when they witness bullying. In a virtual environment, it also means reaching out to parents and teachers in instances of cyberbullying.

Middle School Level

Create a digital citizenship pledge campaign for your students. Work with the students to design a poster of the pledge campaign that will be signed by all students and hung in a highly visible place in your classroom.

High School Level

At this stage, your students will have an understanding of what it means to be a good digital citizen, so it is the perfect time to put their knowledge to use in a positive, meaningful way. Help them find a cause, charity, or actionable event that they can be a part of to make a positive impact in the digital world. Encourage them to find a cause they are passionate about and make a public service announcement (PSA) that will be seen by their fellow students.

Suggestions

Take advantage of the plethora of online resources for educators. You don't need to reinvent the wheel. There are many lesson plans, videos, tutorials, and curriculum ideas found through trusted, online sources.

Don't be afraid to share the negative model so your students can clearly see where the defined boundaries of digital citizenship lie.

FUTURE-READY **DETAILS**

---•

Digital Age Skills Used

- Digital Literacy
- Citizenship
- Information Literacy

ISTE Standards Addressed

- Global Collaborator
- Digital Citizen
- Knowledge Constructor

Reflection

1. In what ways did this challenge change/influence my teaching style? How have my students and I benefited from this change?

2. In what ways did the challenge change the way my classroom functions? How did this improve the learning process?

3. How did the use of technology and digital resources facilitate the implementation of this challenge in my classroom? Which resources were the most effective? How can I use these resources to further develop and advance my curriculum?

Bringing Superheroes to Life

During technology literacy classes at South Fayette Intermediate School, two topics that students learn about are digital citizenship and computational thinking through computer programming. One of my favorite ways to explore concepts of digital citizenship is through the creative process.

After discussing digital citizenship with my students, I ask them to create interactive computer animations in Scratch to demonstrate to others how to be safe, responsible, and respectful online.

I also use the Super Digital Citizen lesson from Common Sense Media that uses Spiderman's motto, "With great power comes great responsibility." We discuss the power that the internet gives them and the ways they can stay safe, responsible, and respectful online.

Students use Google Slides to create design journals so they can reflect upon their learning and to plan out projects. In their design journals, students brainstorm and then write a brief description of a digital citizen superhero—similar to your common everyday superhero, but their powers are used to help people stay safe, responsible, and respectful online.

Once they have created their superhero's backstory, students go to the Marvel Comics website to create their superhero. They copy and paste a screenshot of their comic book creation into their design journal. Next, they storyboard a "digital dilemma," having their digital superhero save the day by helping an internet user learn an important digital citizenship tip. They draw their story like a comic strip, take a digital picture of it, and add it to their design journal.

Once they have their comic strip storyboarded, they learn the programming basics they need to know in order to create an interactive animation in Scratch. Students practice working with characters, or sprites as they are known in Scratch. *Creative Computing: An Introductory Computing Curriculum Using Scratch* is the guide used for these lessons. Students learn to program two or more sprites to carry on a conversation.

Then they write their own script as part of the Talking Safely Online lesson from Common Sense Media and program sprites to talk to each other. They learn how to change backgrounds in Scratch in order to create a setting for their animation. Then they go online to import backgrounds from Google image searches, always remembering to give credit for using other people's work. Students write programming code to switch scenes and show and hide characters.

Finally, they bring it all together. Referring back to their design journals, students copy, paste, and edit their digital citizen superheroes as a sprite in their Scratch animation. Their comic strip storyboard is brought to life as sprites and backgrounds are added, and dialogue between characters helps tell their stories. Students add their projects to an online studio and offer feedback to one another.

Just saying "I like this" is not enough; their critique should provide suggestions for improvement. A final reflection is added to their design journals. Through the reflection questions in their design journal and peer feedback within Scratch, students assess and monitor the quality of their own work against the assessment criteria rubric and their classmates' projects. In the end, the digital citizen superheroes save the day and students do their part to help make the internet a better place for everyone.

Shad Wachter, Fifth Grade Technology
South Fayette Intermediate School, South Fayette Township School District
McDonald, Pennsylvania

WEEK 15

EMPOWER STUDENT VOICE

Student-centered learning moves students from passive receivers of information to active participants in their own discovery process. What students learn, how they learn it and how their learning is assessed are all driven by each individual student's needs and abilities.

—ISTE ESSENTIAL CONDITIONS, 2016

I t's an age-old concept that seems rather logical. But we've strayed from this concept and have become a teacher-centered system. For years, teachers have taught the way they learn, and the way they were taught. But this type of teaching accomplishes little and certainly does not prepare our digital age learners for success.

Instead, we need to make the student the center of attention once again and *teach the way they learn*. We must put the student at the center of every question we ask, every decision we make, every policy a school board creates.

In order to create a student-centered classroom, building, and district, we must always keep our focus on the students and work toward making every decision, every action with them in mind.

For example, the food services manager is in charge of choosing the school lunch menu for the month. Is he making his decisions based on cost effectiveness for the district or on student health and student interest? Who should be driving the decisions? In a student-centered building, the decisions of the food services manager would be made with the students as the central focus. It's all about shifting the cultural mindset to focus on the needs of the students.

In your classroom, you can begin making the shift by considering that students learn in different ways, so teaching them the way you were taught or how you learn best may not be in the best interest of your students. You may be an auditory learner and therefore tend to teach in the auditory style, but if you have a class of visual learners, you likely are not reaching them. Remember: It's about the students sitting in front of you!

It's a hard pill to swallow—and it's a hard change to make, because this change is asking you to stray from your comfort zone. It is also one that was likely never brought to your attention!

As a student-centered teacher, you will take the needs of your students into account before anything else.

For example, three-quarters of your students know the grammar words for the week and are prepared to take the test. In a teacher-centered classroom, you may use another day of study on the grammar words to take into account the remaining one-quarter of the students who do not know the material. However, in a student-centered classroom, you will engage all of your students at their level. This means you will allow the majority of students who know the content to dive deeper into a concept while you provide the remaining students with the additional instruction they need.

This differentiation of instruction may be accomplished through enrichment activities, learning stations, small-group learning, and so on. Your goal in student-centered learning is to ensure that all of your students are being challenged at all times.

According to Carol Ann Tomlinson and Susan Demirsky Allan's *Leadership for Differentiating Schools & Classrooms* (2000), educators can accomplish differentiated instruction using the following principles:

- A differentiated classroom is flexible.

- Differentiation stems from effective and ongoing assessment of learner needs.

- Flexible grouping helps ensure student access to a wide variety of learning opportunities and working arrangements.

- All students consistently work with "respectful" activities and learning arrangements.

- Students and teachers are collaborators in learning.

Challenge

Spend the next week reviewing your teaching style. Consider adding new instructional strategies to make your day as student-centered as possible, such as:

- Flexible grouping—Grouping students together according to similar readiness or learning styles

- Independent study—Creating opportunities for advanced levels of study/inquiry for students who have mastered the content

- Tiered activities—Creating tasks/assignments/projects that vary in complexity

- Learning centers—Providing stations that allow students to explore topics on their own

Reflection

1. In what ways did this challenge change/influence my teaching style? How have my students and I benefited from this change?

2. In what ways did the challenge change the way my classroom functions? How did this improve the learning process?

3. How did the use of technology and digital resources facilitate the implementation of this challenge in my classroom? Which resources were the most effective? How can I use these resources to further develop and advance my curriculum?

WEEK 16

CREATE STUDENT SCHOLARS

You can teach a student a lesson for a day; but if you can teach him to learn by creating curiosity, he will continue the learning process as long as he lives.

—CLAY P. BEDFORD

W e know that in order to fully engage our digital age learners, we need to make them part of the learning process. This means that we must allow our students to take charge of their own learning, essentially creating student *scholars*.

The term *scholar* refers to a person who has advanced knowledge or who has completed an advanced level of study in a particular field.

From an educator's perspective, student scholars are allowed to dictate their instruction based on their needs, their interests, and their passions, often through digital inquiry. Student scholars are able to identify their passions and further explore them with the right digital tools.

The whole idea of an uncertain future lends itself to the student scholar and to allowing students to dictate their futures. We must help our digital age learners go beyond us to become scholarly experts in a topic that may not even exist yet!

One of the best ways to incorporate the concept of creating student scholars is through Joy Kirr and Tom Driscoll's 20-Time in Education model (20timeineducation.com), later combined with the concept of Genius Hour. This model allows students to spend an hour per week working on an independent project of their choice. How you choose to create, design, and direct your Genius Hour is up to you. Some teachers ask students to spend at least 20 minutes of that time reading or researching using digital resources, while other teachers ask students to create a focus or ask an essential question to guide their Genius Hour. Genius Hour fulfills the need our digital age students have for autonomous, inquiry-based learning experiences.

Challenge

Find the passion within your students and help them become student scholars.

Example

Elementary School Level

It may be difficult for your students to identify their interests and passions at this age, so help them along by having them complete interest surveys. (Scholastic has a host of surveys you can print at https://printables.scholastic.com.) Ask them to create a mini research project based on their chosen interest.

Middle School Level

Ask students to identify their interests and then find occupations that revolve around that interest. From there they choose an occupation and perform a deep-rooted investigation into how that occupation complements their passion.

High School Level

Create professional shadowing opportunities for your students. Have them bring their experiences and related research to you and their fellow students, allowing them to essentially become the resident expert on that topic or profession.

FUTURE-READY DETAILS

Digital Age Skills Used	ISTE Standards Addressed
• Creativity	• Empowered Learner
• Innovation	• Creative Communicator
• Leadership	• Knowledge Constructor
	• Innovative Designer

Suggestions

Don't allow your opinion to sway your student's inquiries. Allow them to explore their interests and passions without fear of judgment.

Ensure that you are helping your students find appropriate digital resources to keep them safe while exploring their interests.

Reflection

1. In what ways did this challenge change/influence my teaching style? How have my students and I benefited from this change?

2. In what ways did the challenge change the way my classroom functions? How did this improve the learning process?

3. How did the use of technology and digital resources facilitate the implementation of this challenge in my classroom? Which resources were the most effective? How can I use these resources to further develop and advance my curriculum?

CASE STUDY   +++

Student-Driven Literature Circles

Students love interacting with their peers. Literature circles allow me to use my students' need for socialization to transform my 90-minute reading block.

I first introduce literature circles by asking a simple, open-ended question: "What is a literature circle?" Their reply, "When we sit in a circle and discuss books." I agreed with their interpretation and told them it was even more involved as I explained more about the parts of a literature circle.

In literature circles, the class is divided into reading groups, with each group consisting of four or five students. Each group can select its own book to read or the class can choose one book. While reading their selected book, students complete various "jobs" emphasizing skills such as high-level questioning, vocabulary development, and writing. During the literature circle, students can share their jobs with their peers and engage in lively discussions about the book they are reading. I used Brent Coley's literature circle assignment sheets (www.brentcoley.com).

I show my students some videos to pique their interest and explain the "jobs" to them. (There are many great literature examples on YouTube.) After practicing the strategy as a class, I divide students into their groups and then let them choose their first assignment/job.

I trust the process and communicate to my students that I believed they can take responsibility of their learning. I listen to their discussions and intervene only when invited or when necessary because of problems.

I increase their motivation and need for my approval by displaying their work in the classroom for other groups and classes to see. A student suggested I choose which work to display by allowing some friendly competition.

Continued

My students often say things such as, "I can't believe it's time to go already," or "This class goes by so quickly." Their engagement and investment in the process increases, which thereby increases their motivation to read and do their 'job' so they won't let anyone in their circle down.

Amy Pryor, Reading Specialist, M.A.
Title I, New Manchester Elementary, Hancock County School District
New Cumberland, West Virginia

GRADING—THE BIG CHANGE

Grades are "relics from a less enlightened age."

—ALFIE KOHN

L et me pose a question: If you took a course and the teacher gave you a ◆ or a ■ at the end of the course, what would it mean to you? Would the chosen symbol reflect how well you did in the course or provide you with any information?

Unfortunately, our grading system is nothing more than useless symbols. Nowhere in that A, B, C, D, or F does it reveal if the child has mastered the skill or whether the child is prepared to move on.

Our current grading system must change! We must move beyond the competitive grade letters we use today to a more modern approach that better indicates if our children have successfully mastered a skill or a concept. Our children's ability to take a test gives absolutely no indication of whether they will remember it six months from now. Yes, our current method of assessing and grading students must change!

For true digital age students, letter grades mean little and certainly don't indicate whether they possess the concepts necessary to progress into an unknown future. When they enter the real world, it won't matter if they got an A or B; instead, it will matter if they have the skills necessary to be competitive in the digital age job market.

To become the educators our digital age students need, we must assess their mastery of a skill through real-world use of that skill, as opposed to a flat, test-type assessment. There will never be a time in their adult lives when they will be given a problem to solve and then shown five possible answers—one of which must be right! It doesn't work in our world, and it certainly won't work in the future.

We must find ways to assess a student's understanding in a real-world format, such as project-based learning. We need to put into motion assessments that say, "Do this and show me you understand." We must prepare our students for the real world, not a world of testing.

If we don't place a letter or number grade on learning, we can embrace the skills and continue to practice them until mastery is achieved (Sackstein, 2015).

Challenge

Spend this week not giving ONE grade! Instead, consider implementing the following:

In lieu of a letter grade on the next assignment, have a short, one-on-one student conference. Ask your students how they feel in terms of their mastery of the skill and then provide them your interpretation of the said skill or concept. Imagine how a meaningful dialogue on a weekly basis will open up communication between you and your students!

Consider recording an audio or video dialogue regarding each student's progress and send it to their parents to keep lines of communication open, not only between you and your students but also between students and parents and you and parents.

Reflection

1. In what ways did this challenge change/influence my teaching style? How have my students and I benefited from this change?

2. In what ways did the challenge change the way my classroom functions? How did this improve the learning process?

3. How did the use of technology and digital resources facilitate the implementation of this challenge in my

classroom? Which resources were the most effective? How can I use these resources to further develop and advance my curriculum?

LOOKING TO THE FUTURE

Children are likely to live up to what
you believe of them.

—LADY BIRD JOHNSON

Congratulations! With a school semester under your belt, you are wiser, more creative, more enlightened, and more devoted to your digital age learners than ever. You have made meaningful changes to your classroom, which have resulted in extraordinary changes in your students' lives.

Each day you ask yourself, "Am I doing the best I can possibly do for my students?" You are the molder, the builder of your students' lives, and you know that what you create in your students will determine what the future will look like.

It's not always easy to design and implement dynamic, creative lessons, and it's certainly not easy to take the time to understand what your students need and then deliver on those needs. But you didn't get into teaching because it was easy! You did it to make a difference in children's lives. You live compassion, enthusiasm, dedication, and steadfastness every day, and your students reap the rewards.

Your passion for teaching today's digital age learners to prepare them for tomorrow's world—a world we cannot even begin to envision—places you in a unique position to change how the future unfolds. It also firmly positions you as a member of one of the most powerful groups in the world!

You've finished *The Future-Ready Challenge* and are now ready to take what you've learned and begin making significant changes to your curriculum as you head into the second semester of the school year.

But before you dive headfirst into your second semester, armed with an arsenal of techniques, plans, and ideas for nurturing and supporting your digital age learners, take the time to reflect on the hits, misses, successes, and challenges of the last 18 weeks.

Challenge

Reflect, Respect, and Direct.

Reflect on your 18 weeks' worth of experiences. What did you learn about yourself? What did you learn about your students?

Do you feel that you have become a better teacher? Which digital age skills were the easiest to implement? Which ones were the most difficult? What can I do to better incorporate those skills into my curriculum? If you do then, *Respect.* Take care of yourself this week and celebrate your amazing accomplishments. You should be proud of what you did and why you did it, for the good of your students. Finally, *Direct.* You must now spread the word. Take what you have learned from this challenge and get more involved. Get at least five people involved in having their own 18-week challenge with you as their mentor, their model—their 21st-century educator.

Reflection

1. In what ways did the challenges change/influence my teaching style? How have my students and I benefited from these changes?

2. In what ways did the challenges change the way my classroom functions? How did this improve the learning process?

3. Which digital age skills were the easiest to implement? Which ones were the most difficult? What can I do to better incorporate those skills into my curriculum?

4. How did the use of technology and digital resources facilitate the implementation of these challenges in my classroom? Which resources were the most effective? How can I use these resources to further develop and advance my curriculum?

Conclusion

You've successfully completed your 18-week challenge. But wait—there's one challenge left, perhaps the most important challenge of all: continue what you're doing. Take what you've learned to the next level. As educators, we know that many times the person doing the teaching is also doing the learning. Your final challenge is to make a conscience effort to adopt these challenges so they become part of your teaching philosophy.

Your commitment to implementing digital age skills makes you part of an exciting, grassroots teaching movement. Sounds odd, doesn't it? Working with these skills in mind, you are designing new and exciting ways to teach your students. You are engaging your students in a creative, meaningful way and equipping them with skills that will follow them throughout their educational journey and into adulthood.

Digital age skills may sound forward-thinking, but the concepts are anything but. We may have an abundance of technology and tools to make the experience exciting and engaging, but if you boil it down, these skills are nothing new—still, they've never been more important!

We are preparing our students for the unknown, for jobs and careers of the future. Instilling the tried-and-true, time-tested soft skills of collaboration, communication, and critical thinking will help them be able to tackle the challenges that await them.

Go to your past for a moment and think about some of your superhero teachers—those educators who grabbed your attention, flipped the antiquated teaching script, and inspired you to become an educator yourself. I guarantee you they were already masters of these future-ready skills. Take what you've learned, move forward with confidence, and become the superhero teacher your students deserve.

REFERENCES

American Management Association. (2010). *AMA 2010 Critical Skills Survey.* Retrieved from http://www.amanet.org/news/AMA-2010-critical-skills-survey.aspx

Association for Career and Technical Education, National Association of State Directors of Career Technical Education Consortium and Partnership for 21st Century Skills. (2010). *Up to the challenge: The role of career and technical education and 21st century skills in college and career readiness.* Retrieved from http://www.p21.org/storage/documents/CTE_Oct2010.pdf

Davis, M. (2016). *What is digital citizenship?* Retrieved from https://edtechdigest.wordpress.com/2016/06/15/what-is-digital-citizenship/

GDC Team. (n.d.). *The critical 21st century skills every student needs and why.* Global Digital Citizen Foundation. Retrieved from https://globaldigitalcitizen.org/21st-century-skills-every-student-needs

Great Schools Partnership. (2014). *The glossary of education reform: 21st century skills.* Retrieved from http://edglossary.org/21st-century-skills/

Heick, T. (2013). *The definition of digital citizenship.* Retrieved from www.teachthought.com/the-future-of-learning/digital-citizenship-the-future-of-learning/the-definition-of-digital-citzenship/

International Reading Association/ National Council of Teachers of English. (2004). *Peer edit with perfection.* Retrieved from www.readwritethink.org/resources/resource-print.html?id=786

Maltz, M. (1989). *Psycho-cybernetics.* New York, NY: Simon & Schuster.

Meyer, A. E. (1967). *An educational history of the American people.* New York, NY: McGraw-Hill.

Meyerson, B. (2015, March 4). Top 10 emerging technologies of 2015. *Scientific American.* Retrieved from http://www.scientificamerican.com/article/top-10-emerging-technologies-of-20151/

National Education Association. (n.d.). *Preparing 21st century students for a global society: An educator's guide to the "Four Cs".* Retrieved from http://www.nea.org/assets/docs/A-Guide-to-Four-Cs.pdf

Nelson, B. (2012). *The real definition of entrepreneur---And why it matters.* Retrieved from www.forbes.com/sites/brettnelson/2012/06/05/the-real-definition-of-entrepreneur-and-why-it-matters/#6c10709571ae

Pink, D. H. (2005). *A whole new mind: Moving from the informational age to the conceptual age.* New York, NY: Riverhead Books.

Ribble, M. (2017). *Nine elements.* Retrieved from http://digitalcitizenship.net/Nine_Elements.html

Ribble, M., & Bailey, G. (2007). *Digital citizenship in schools.* Eugene, OR: ISTE.

Sackstein, S. (2015). *Still not convinced grades are bad?* Retrieved from http://blogs.edweek.org/teachers/work_in_progress/2015/03/still_not_convinced_grades_are.html

Thoughtful Learning. (2017). *What are 21st century skills?* Retrieved from https://k12.thoughtfullearning.com/FAQ/what-are-21st-century-skills

Tomlinson, C.A., & Allen, S.D. (2000). *Leadership for Differentiating Schools & Classrooms.* Alexandria, VA: Association for Supervision & Curriculum Development.

Tyler, R. W. (1949). *Basic principles of curriculum and instruction.* Chicago, IL: University of Chicago Press.

Wiggins, G., & McTighe, J. (2005). *Understanding by design.* Alexandria, VA: Association for Supervision & Curriculum Development.

World Economic Forum. (2015). *New vision for education: Unlocking the potential of technology.* World Economic Forum. Retrieved from http://www3.weforum.org/docs/WEFUSA_NewVisionforEducation_Report2015.pdf

ISTE STANDARDS

2016 ISTE Standards for Students

The 2016 ISTE Standards for Students emphasize the skills and qualities we want for students, enabling them to engage and thrive in a connected, digital world. The standards are designed for use by educators across the curriculum, with every age student, with a goal of cultivating these skills throughout a student's academic career. Both students and teachers will be responsible for achieving foundational technology skills to fully apply the standards. The reward, however, will be educators who skillfully mentor and inspire students to amplify learning with technology and challenge them to be agents of their own learning.

1. **Empowered Learner**

   Students leverage technology to take an active role in choosing, achieving and demonstrating competency in their learning goals, informed by the learning sciences. Students:

   a. articulate and set personal learning goals, develop strategies leveraging technology to achieve them and reflect on the learning process itself to improve learning outcomes.

   b. build networks and customize their learning environments in ways that support the learning process.

   c. use technology to seek feedback that informs and improves their practice and to demonstrate their learning in a variety of ways.

    d. understand the fundamental concepts of technology operations, demonstrate the ability to choose, use and troubleshoot current technologies and are able to transfer their knowledge to explore emerging technologies.

2. **Digital Citizen**

   Students recognize the rights, responsibilities and opportunities of living, learning and working in an interconnected digital world, and they act and model in ways that are safe, legal and ethical. Students:

       a. cultivate and manage their digital identity and reputation and are aware of the permanence of their actions in the digital world.

       b. engage in positive, safe, legal and ethical behavior when using technology, including social interactions online or when using networked devices.

       c. demonstrate an understanding of and respect for the rights and obligations of using and sharing intellectual property.

       d. manage their personal data to maintain digital privacy and security and are aware of data-collection technology used to track their navigation online.

3. **Knowledge Constructor**

   Students critically curate a variety of resources using digital tools to construct knowledge, produce creative artifacts and make meaningful learning experiences for themselves and others. Students:

a. plan and employ effective research strategies to locate information and other resources for their intellectual or creative pursuits.

b. evaluate the accuracy, perspective, credibility and relevance of information, media, data or other resources.

c. curate information from digital resources using a variety of tools and methods to create collections of artifacts that demonstrate meaningful connections or conclusions.

d. build knowledge by actively exploring real-world issues and problems, developing ideas and theories and pursuing answers and solutions.

4. **Innovative Designer**

Students use a variety of technologies within a design process to identify and solve problems by creating new, useful or imaginative solutions. Students:

a. know and use a deliberate design process for generating ideas, testing theories, creating innovative artifacts or solving authentic problems.

b. select and use digital tools to plan and manage a design process that considers design constraints and calculated risks.

c. develop, test and refine prototypes as part of a cyclical design process.

d. exhibit a tolerance for ambiguity, perseverance and the capacity to work with open-ended problems.

5. **Computational Thinker**

Students develop and employ strategies for understanding and solving problems in ways that leverage the power of technological methods to develop and test solutions. Students:

   a. formulate problem definitions suited for technology-assisted methods such as data analysis, abstract models and algorithmic thinking in exploring and finding solutions.

   b. collect data or identify relevant data sets, use digital tools to analyze them, and represent data in various ways to facilitate problem-solving and decision-making.

   c. break problems into component parts, extract key information, and develop descriptive models to understand complex systems or facilitate problem-solving.

   d. understand how automation works and use algorithmic thinking to develop a sequence of steps to create and test automated solutions.

6. **Creative Communicator**

Students communicate clearly and express themselves creatively for a variety of purposes using the platforms, tools, styles, formats and digital media appropriate to their goals. Students:

   a. choose the appropriate platforms and tools for meeting the desired objectives of their creation or communication.

b. create original works or responsibly repurpose or remix digital resources into new creations.

c. communicate complex ideas clearly and effectively by creating or using a variety of digital objects such as visualizations, models or simulations.

d. publish or present content that customizes the message and medium for their intended audiences.

7. **Global Collaborator**

Students use digital tools to broaden their perspectives and enrich their learning by collaborating with others and working effectively in teams locally and globally. Students:

a. use digital tools to connect with learners from a variety of backgrounds and cultures, engaging with them in ways that broaden mutual understanding and learning.

b. use collaborative technologies to work with others, including peers, experts or community members, to examine issues and problems from multiple viewpoints.

c. contribute constructively to project teams, assuming various roles and responsibilities to work effectively toward a common goal.

d. explore local and global issues and use collaborative technologies to work with others to investigate solutions.